THE EMOTIONAL COST OF CLARITY

How Burnout, Boundaries, and Breakdowns Lead to Breakthroughs

SHANTE ALEXANDER, MA,PCC

Copyright © 2026 by SHANTE ALEXANDER
All rights reserved.

No part of this publication may be reproduced, stored in a retrieval system, or transmitted in any form or by any means, electronic, mechanical, photocopying, recording, scanning, or otherwise, without the prior written permission of the author.

Limit of Liability/Disclaimer of Warranty: While the publisher and author have used their best efforts in preparing this book, they make no representations or warranties with respect to the accuracy or completeness of the contents of this book and specifically disclaim any implied warranties of merchantability or fitness for a particular purpose. No warranty may be created or extended by sales representatives or written sales materials. The advice and strategies contained herein may not be suitable for your situation. You should consult with a professional when appropriate. Neither the publisher nor the author shall be liable for any loss of profit or any other commercial damages, including but not limited to special, incidental, consequential, personal, or other damages. Some names and identifying details of people described in this book have been altered to protect their privacy.

The Emotional Cost of Clarity:
How Burnout, Boundaries and Breakdowns Lead to Breakthroughs
by Shante Alexander

PSYCHOLOGY / Interpersonal Relations
SELF-HELP / Personal Growth / General
PSYCHOLOGY / Industrial & Organizational Psychology

ISBN 979-8-9941976-0-8 (paperback)
ISBN 979-8-9941976-1-5 (ebook)

Edited by Robin Schroffel
Cover and Interior Layout by JBookDesigns

Printed in the United States of America

Positive Transitions Coaching & Consulting LLC
New York, NY 10037

DEDICATION

To the one who kept showing up — even when you weren't sure who you were showing up as.

To the one who kept pouring from an empty place — giving until you finally whispered, *"Something has to give."*

To the one who's been mislabeled, misunderstood, underestimated, or overstretched, you held on and endured.
You've been told you're too sensitive, too strong, too quiet, too small, or too much — yet you're still here.

Picking up this book shows you're willing to challenge the status quo. That choice alone takes courage.

Your burnout spoke first.
Your breakdowns revealed the truth.
And the cracks you tried to hide have become the openings leading you toward clarity.

This is for you — honoring not just where you've been, but also the possibility of who you are becoming.

**With clarity,
Shante**

CONTENTS

Introduction: The Cost of Seeing Clearly vii

🔒 Section One: Guarded Giving™

Chapter 1: Guarded Giving 5
Chapter 2: Building Boundaries 34
Chapter 3: Redefining Love 54
Chapter 4: Respect and Self-Betrayal 78

🎭 Section Two: Fake Sincerity

Chapter 5: Emotional Availability and the Fear of Being Felt 118
Chapter 6: Gratitude and Resentment 149
Chapter 7: Performative Connection 173
Chapter 8: Emotional Safety and Intimacy 200

⬢ Section Three: Isolating Reconnection

Chapter 9: Isolating Reconnection 231
Chapter 10: The Space in Between 252
Chapter 11: Discerning Forgiveness 270
Chapter 12: The Mirror and the Mountain 301
A Final Letter to You 319

INTRODUCTION
THE COST OF SEEING CLEARLY

This isn't a self-help book. It's a self-honoring book that offers a unique perspective on personal and professional growth and healing.

Having coached hundreds of high-achieving professionals, I've discovered a sobering truth: many of their so-called "strengths" are actually born from survival instincts. Traits such as work ethic, perfectionism, over-performance, and resilience aren't always driven by joy or purpose—they often result from trauma conditioning. This doesn't diminish their success, but it does add complexity to their stories.

This understanding of common high-performance traits explains why traditional self-help, which often depends on superficial or quick fixes, usually fails. These books typically claim that life can improve through affirmations and simple strategies, but they frequently ignore the discomfort that clarity can bring. Quick solutions can't heal wounds built up over the years. Genuine clarity requires facing uncomfortable truths. Healing demands effort and sincere self-exploration, not just motivation. This book isn't about shortcuts; it will guide you through the hard, honest work needed to find alignment. It recognizes that disconnection isn't necessarily a flaw but a natural response to systems, roles, and seasons that no longer serve you.

I remember opening one of those brightly colored, promising self-help books with a highlighter in hand, only to feel a hollowness settle in. Page after page, I was told to "push harder," "be grateful," or "manifest more," as if the weight I carried proved my own weakness. The questions didn't go deep enough, and the answers were less meaningful. I didn't want to pretend I had it all together—I actually wanted to *get it* together. I wanted to grow and heal. That's why so many of those books still sit unfinished on my shelves. Now they serve as reminders of how invisible I felt in spaces that were meant to speak to me. That's not what this book is.

The Emotional Cost of Clarity was never meant to be a motivational speech. It's not intended to boost your productivity or sugarcoat your pain. It's here to name what you've been quietly carrying. To hold space for the unlearning, uncertainty, and uneasiness that clarity often brings. We will acknowledge the very real sense of grief that comes with this process. This grief, raw and unsettling, usually emerges as we shed old identities and familiar patterns. It's the undoing that must happen before any of the "feel-good" breakthroughs occur.

Because the truth is, more often than not, breakthroughs come with significant turbulence. Sometimes they arrive on the plane of loss, resentment, burnout, and breakdowns. This book is a witness to that process. It doesn't skip the messy middle—because that's where your realignment begins, centering on your personal journey. It doesn't pretend the path is straight—because growth rarely is. It doesn't try to fix what's broken. It honors the breaking—and the clarity that begins to rebuild afterward.

As an organizational psychologist, coach, and someone who has experienced personal and professional seasons of misalignment, I created this for those who are outgrowing who they've become but are still unsure about who they *will* become. If that describes you, you're in the right place. Welcome to the pause before your pivot—the mirror before the movement. The quiet reckoning before taking the next right step. This book aims to help you **name it, normalize it, and navigate it.**

With clarity,
Shante

SECTION ONE
GUARDED GIVING™

When you've learned to give to others but not to yourself.

TO THE ONE WHO BELIEVED BEING NEEDED EQUALED BEING VALUED

You gave and gave—until giving became your identity.

Connection was built on what you could do, solve, carry, or fix. And when you couldn't . . . the silence was louder than any praise ever was. You believed being needed meant you mattered, and that usefulness equaled love.

But now, with clarity, you've started to untangle that lie. You've realized that unbalanced giving taught you to anticipate everyone's needs but your own. Eventually, you began avoiding even the people you loved most, not because you didn't care for them, but because you were drained from constantly giving.

Isolating was the only way you knew how to set boundaries. You didn't know any other way to handle the pressure of what people expected from you. That's when you started giving cautiously. But this kind of giving comes from fear, anxiety, and a lack of trust. As a result, you felt guilty, which made you feel like the villain for not showing up. With clarity, you know:

- Being needed isn't the same as being appreciated.
- Being selfless doesn't mean fading away.
- Saying no isn't rejection; it's acknowledgment.

You're still learning how to express your limitations and standards. Still figuring out how to say, "I love you, but I don't have the capacity." Still learning to trust that your voice matters as much as your presence. By unlearning Guarded Giving, you can begin to heal and become a more accessible and open person. You'll realize that the version of you who gives but hides, and the one that doesn't feel obligated to say "yes," still deserves to be seen.

With clarity,
Shante

CHAPTER 1
GUARDED GIVING

You're not flaky. You're exhausted from constantly being needed.

You've been the strong one for so long that it feels strange to imagine another way. The dependable one. The capable one. The one who keeps giving—because you always have. But somewhere along the way, giving became the only way you know how to survive. You're exhausted from constantly being needed, but you don't know how to turn it off.

You've mastered the art of showing up, even when you're running on fumes. People trust your reliability, your empathy, and your ability to make things happen. But beneath that competence lives a quiet fatigue—the kind that comes from being everyone's safe place and rarely having one yourself.

This chapter isn't about generosity; it's about survival disguised as generosity. It explores how over-giving, over-functioning, and over-accommodating often grow from unhealed wounds and a longing to feel worthy. *Guarded Giving* is the armor worn by those who love deeply but have been hurt before—those who confuse being needed with being loved, and find it hard to ask for their own essentials to be met.

You became dependable, resourceful, and strong. But somewhere along the way, your giving became guarded. Your kindness was filtered through exhaustion. Your yes started to mean "I guess," as if you had no real choice.

"If my giving doesn't give me joy, I'm giving the wrong way."

This is a clarity statement I've coined and seek to live by. It helps me manage my activities and ensure I'm giving in the most sustainable way possible. It's based on a very popular quote. Fill in the blank: *"For there is more happiness in _____."*

It's a well-known verse—quoted often, rarely examined. We nod at the idea that "there is more happiness in giving than there is in receiving," yet overlook the truth hidden inside it: real giving is meant to *refresh*, not *drain*. True generosity inherently carries reciprocity—not the transactional kind, but the nourishing kind. The kind that leaves both giver and receiver restored and happy. If your giving leaves you bitter, empty, or unseen, it's no longer generosity—it's depletion dressed up as virtue. It's performance disguised as purpose. And while the world might praise it, your soul can't sustain it.

*　*　*

Defining Guarded Giving

Guarded Giving is the act of offering care, time, or vulnerability while keeping your emotional armor in place—because past experiences have shown you that connection often comes at a cost. It's the habit of showing up even when you're empty, because saying no feels like failure. It's the performance of strength when what you really need is rest.

It looks like:

- Deliberate distancing that appears flaky.
- Self-isolation masked as "being busy."
- Energetic generosity layered with emotional restraint or distance.

Think:

✔ You give—but only when it feels safe. You respond to others' needs with generosity, yet often stay unaware of their lives until a request arrives. Your care shows up in action, not initiation.

✔ You care deeply—sometimes without realizing it. People may not sense your affection until you step in to help; your love often hides behind doing rather than being.

✔ You connect—with caution. You've been conditioned to expect that most people reach out to you when they need something, not simply to nurture a connection—so you avoid reaching out too. It's self-protection, not apathy.

Guarded Giving is what happens when love and obligation intertwine. It's giving with one hand while keeping the other braced for disappointment. It's not coldness—it's conditioning. It's the learned survival mode for people who have spent years being praised for their coerced martyrdom—confusing depletion for devotion.

How Guarded Giving Begins

Guarded Giving doesn't start as a flaw—it begins as protection. Somewhere along the line, you learned that being available made you useful, and being useful made you safe. Approval became your currency. So you offered yourself in pieces—helping, fixing, showing up—until generosity became your language of survival.

At first, it felt good. You were appreciated. Needed. Valued. But the praise was conditional, and the safety was temporary. Love had terms. Worth had proof. And silence felt safer than saying, "I'm tired."

Every act of giving built trust with others—but chipped away at trust with yourself. That's how Guarded Giving takes root: not from coldness, but from **an identity shaped by sanctioned self-betrayal.** Guarded Giving may appear generous, but its roots often run deeper than kindness. It's not just *how* you give—it's *why*.

In striving to express love in an unselfish, principled way, wisdom must walk hand in hand with compassion. Even the purest motives can become distorted when love isn't balanced with discernment. You can care so deeply that you forget to come up for air—be so devoted to doing good that you quietly self-destruct. Real love does not require collapse to prove its sincerity.

True, unselfish love requires knowledge, humility, and divine wisdom for its proper expression. It must be guided by principles that are already true and established—not ones invented to excuse harm or justify comfort. Principles such as honesty, reciprocity, and respect for free will have anchored love across cultures and time, as they honor both truth and humanity. Love without those guiding truths becomes sentiment without structure.

As Amy Carmichael wrote, "You can give without loving, but you cannot love without giving." Love, when aligned with wisdom, gives from integrity—not obligation. It acts with compassion *and* ownership. Each of the four facets of love—**eros, storge, philia, and agape**—has the potential to create profound joy. But only when that love is anchored in enduring principles—truth, integrity, and compassion—can it bring real happiness and peace.

* * *

The Motive Behind the Giving

> *"You can give without loving, but you cannot love without giving."* —Amy Carmichael.

Not all giving comes from the same place. Some of it is driven by joy, but much of it is influenced by motives we haven't thoroughly examined. Giving may bring you joy because it aligns with your values and allows you to express love for others. However, you might also give to avoid conflict, to protect an image, because you believe your worth is tied to what you do, or to maintain a connection at your own expense.

The challenge—and the chance—is to pause long enough to ask: *Is this choice driven by clarity or by need? By stewardship or by fear?* Recognizing why you give is the first step in changing how you give. When the motive is tangled in fear, guilt, approval, or avoidance, it's no longer generosity—it's armor. And armor, no matter how shiny, remains heavy.

When you start examining why you give, the truth can be disarming. Some of our most celebrated traits—loyalty, dependability, service—can hide the quiet desperation to be seen as good, capable, or worthy. We call it purpose, but sometimes it's survival. We pour until we're empty, then apologize for the mess.

💬 Client Vignette: When "I'm Fine" Breaks

I logged in for my very first coaching session with a senior director at a major corporation. She looked the part of a hard-working, competent leader. Excited to dive in and provide leadership coaching, I asked, "How are you today?" and braced for the usual polite exchange. She gave me a half-smile and said, "I'm f—" Before the word could finish, she burst into tears. For several minutes, she cried with a stranger, apologizing between sobs.

She wasn't unprofessional, too sensitive, or unstable—she was *empty*. Not because she was weak, but because years of over-giving, over-functioning, and over-performing had left her without reserves. Guarded Giving had caught up to her, and she had no armor left to hold it in. I wish I could say this was rare. It isn't. In session after session, I've watched the armor of high-achieving men and women fall away the moment they realize that competence has cost them connection.

Sadly, many of us don't even recognize why we developed this armor. For some, it's rooted in attachment patterns. Avoidant patterns often grow from the belief that dependency equals danger—that trusting others will mean losing yourself. So you manage closeness by managing distance. Others might see withdrawal; you experience it as protection—a way to survive intimacy without surrendering your identity. But over time, that same protection becomes prevention—shielding you not only from harm but from the closeness you crave.

So ask yourself: *Why do I give? What values guide my giving? Does the way I give reflect those values—or reject them?*

* * *

The Personal Experience of Guarded Giving

When clarity begins to reach the areas where people-pleasing once resided, you start to notice:

- The roles you've unquestioningly taken on
- The expectations you've let grow unchecked
- The unspoken resentments you've carried

When Honesty Isn't the Same as Being Available

You're the one people say is easy to talk to. You're "real." You're clear. You're open. But emotional honesty doesn't always mean you're emotionally available. You've learned to identify what you feel—but haven't figured out how to maintain a connection without it costing you. So instead of pushing people away, you pause. You pull back. You ration your presence—because presence has started to feel like performance. This pulling back is a protective pattern formed through repeated depletion.

Think:

- You're emotionally honest but relationally unavailable. You can identify what you feel, but still find it challenging to express it in the ways others expect.
- You're not cold or distant. You're still a giver, but you don't have the energy to keep proving it.
- You're not antisocial. You're just . . . socially drained. It's not that you don't want a connection; you can't keep chasing or maintaining it at your own expense.

💬 Personal Reflection: Available and Invisible

I know that fatigue well—the kind that lingers after you've smiled through exhaustion and said, "It's fine, I'm fine," because you don't want the other person to feel bad. For years, I mistook that pattern for strength. Dependability. Faithfulness. I didn't realize it was also my silence saying, *I matter less.*

Guarded Giving isn't born from apathy—it's born from depletion and conditioning that told you, *you don't matter, and your needs are a burden.* It's the quiet rebellion of someone who has given everything but the permission to say no. When you start recognizing that truth, clarity begins to move in—the kind that doesn't just expose what's heavy, but invites you to lay it down.

*　*　*

The Guarded Giving Phase: Before Clarity

When you reflect on the ways you've pulled back from others, can you tell when your distance is protecting your peace—and when it's protecting your pain? Times when space was an act of care—and times when it was a quiet attempt to stay unseen, unheard, or unneeded.

It often shows up as:

- Having trouble articulating your needs
- Avoiding connection out of depletion
- Feeling guilt, conflict, or confusion about setting limits
- Remaining silent instead of expressing what's true

The truth is, guarded giving doesn't always announce itself loudly—it creeps, shaping how you show up in everyday moments. This guardedness doesn't always look dramatic; it often hides in plain sight—inside polite texts, delayed replies, or the subtle hesitation to answer the phone. You may hear the phone ring and think: "If I don't pick up, I don't have to say no."

What this might sound like:

- "Giving is still my nature—I'm just tired of only hearing from people when they want me to be of service."

Sometimes it whispers like (the thoughts you keep to yourself):

- "If I don't pick up, I don't have to say no."

- "I'm not trying to ignore you; I'm trying to avoid the guilt of disappointing you."
- "I crave space and peace—but every time I voice that need, I'm made to feel guilty for it; now, I take the space by shutting down, no warning, just silence."

You start calling it *protecting your peace*, but deep down, you know it's really protecting your pain. That's the part most people won't see—the exhaustion that made silence safer than honesty. Because sometimes the only way to survive being unseen . . . is to stop showing up at all. If you're not going to see me, then at least the disappearance will be on my terms.

That's the illusion of control that softens the ache—deciding when and how the absence happens. It hurts less to withdraw voluntarily than to be dismissed while you're still standing there, open. But even in that retreat, something in you still longs to be understood. That's where the ache of Guarded Giving begins—the craving for connection without the cost.

* * *

The Ache of Wanting Without Burden

Here's the heartbreaking part: You still crave connection. But you want it without the weight, the performance, or the constant pressure to earn your place. You want to be known—but you're afraid that being known means being needed in ways that drain you. And right now, that kind of pressure feels like a job you didn't sign up for—with poor benefits and no PTO.

The truth is, every connection comes with a cost. But there's a difference between an **investment** and an **extraction.**

💡 Reflection Sidebar – Investment Versus Extraction

Every connection costs something. The question is—what kind of cost are you paying?

- **Investment** strengthens what it touches. It may take effort, but it builds trust, mutual care, and emotional safety. You leave interactions with a sense of meaning, not depletion.
- **Extraction** takes more than it gives. It keeps you overextended and underappreciated, confusing loyalty with availability and love with labor.

Healthy connections cost effort. Unhealthy connection costs identity.

Prompt: *Where in your life are you investing your care—and where are you being consumed by obligation?*

It's not selfish to notice where your energy goes—it's honest. But when depletion becomes your default, even discernment begins to dull. You stop evaluating who's safe or aligned and start expecting that every connection will cost you something. So you pull back—not because you don't care, but because you've forgotten what care without cost feels like.

That "coldness" isn't indifference—it's exhaustion and fear disguised as control. Detachment feels safer than discernment because it makes disappointment predictable. Your detachment isn't distance—it's recovery. You're still healing from the ways you practiced giving, the ways you confused love with labor, worth with work, and peace with silence. It's not that you want less love; you want love that honors mutual effort, not exploitation.

The key isn't escaping the cost of connection—it's learning to invest your care where it compounds, not where it depletes. And if you've ever found yourself caught in that space—too drained to reach out, too loyal to walk away—know this: you're not the only one trying to love and protect yourself at the same time.

*　*　*

You're Not Alone, but You're Tired

I used to confuse selflessness with self-worth. If I gave more, helped more, served more, maybe I'd finally feel like enough. On the surface, constantly showing up for others—always saying yes, overextending myself, and sacrificing my own health—seemed admirable. People praised me for being nice, dependable, "the one who's always there." But behind that applause was mismanaged generosity—giving in ways that undermined my well-being because I wasn't using discernment or stewardship. The intent felt pure, but the execution quietly drained me, driven by patterns that sought validation, avoided conflict, and earned my right to be loved.

Over time, I realized service without stewardship isn't generosity—it's self-neglect. It quietly erodes the very self you've been entrusted to guard.

💬 Personal Reflection: Where This Hit Me

I remember the moment it hit me. A friend was sick, so I brought her some food, checked on her kids, and made sure she was okay. Her husband was there, and her mother lived nearby. She had other support options, but I was still called—and I showed up. When I walked the quarter mile back home, I collapsed from exhaustion. Why? Because I was sick too.

It never occurred to me that I could say no. Honestly, I felt like I couldn't. As I lay there, trying to ignore the shame creeping up inside me, I thought about all the other times I'd done the same thing—and how the people around me let me do it. I wish I could say that was my turning point. It wasn't. It took another twenty years to finally see the cost of my giving. Twenty years before I could name it for what it was: a slow, quiet destruction of myself—applauded by others but unsustainable for me.

Maybe you've collapsed in private too, only to pull yourself together before anyone could see the cost.

I can't blame my friend. She asked me to show up in the way I always had—the way that made it look effortless. I was the one who didn't respect my limits. She's still one of my dearest friends.

There's a difference between people who intentionally use you and those who appreciate you because you've conditioned them to believe your capacity is limitless. One takes advantage; the other accepts the version of you you've always offered. The way you tell the difference is by watching how they respond when you start to adjust how you show up.

Those who truly value you will adapt. Those who only valued what you could give them will resist. The real work is learning to tell the difference—and having the courage to honor what that truth reveals.

✍ Reflection Prompt: The Response Reveals the Relationship

Think about the people who have come to expect your presence, help, or energy.

Now ask yourself:

- How do they respond when you begin to slow down, say no, or show up differently?
- Who adapts, gives grace, and honors your limits?

- Who resists, guilts, or withdraws when your giving no longer benefits them?

Write down what you notice. Sometimes clarity isn't about confrontation—it's about observation. The truth reveals itself in how people handle your boundaries, not just how they celebrate your generosity.

* * *

The Hidden Cycle Behind Guarded Giving

⚠ *A Gentle Reminder: I am not a clinical psychologist or medical professional, and the information I share here is not intended to diagnose or treat any medical condition. These words are for reflection, not prescription. If stress, anxiety, panic, meltdowns, or breakdowns feel like a constant companion in your life, I encourage you to seek the care of a licensed mental health professional. You deserve that level of support.*

Stress, burnout, anxiety, panic, meltdowns, and breakdowns. What are they, how are they connected, and how could they affect you? The latest research by the American Psychological Association on stress in America reveals that nearly half of U.S. adults report high levels of stress. And if we're honest, that number is likely much higher—because most of us don't recognize stress until it becomes something harder to ignore.

We can easily spot stress in others but often fail to notice or admit our own. Our bodies adapt to chaos so efficiently that tension, fatigue, and pressure start to feel normal. Many high achievers "manage" stress so well that they mistake survival for strength. But even high-functioning systems eventually wear down. Overworking can mask the body's signals until the whispers become shouts—tight muscles, poor sleep, irritability, and emotional numbness. Recognizing these stages isn't about labeling yourself—it's about noticing what your body and mind have been trying to tell you all along.

Stress (The Activation Stage)

- **What it is:** A physiological and psychological *state of activation* triggered by pressure or demand.
- **Emotions can include:** Irritability, frustration, and worry.
- **Sounds like:** "I'm fine—it's just a busy week. Once I get through this deadline, I'll be okay."
- **Looks like:** You're revved up, tense, and restless. Your system is flooded with adrenaline and cortisol.
- **Outcome:** Stress can motivate (think: the fire under you) or overwhelm (think: the fire consuming you). If managed—through rest, boundaries, or support—it usually passes.

Burnout (The Depletion Stage)

- **What it is:** A state of emotional, physical, and mental exhaustion caused by prolonged, unmanaged stress.
- **Emotions can include:** Numbness, sadness, cynicism, and disillusionment.
- **Sounds like:** "I don't even care anymore. I'm too tired to try."
- **Looks like:** Instead of revved, you're detached, unmotivated, and running on fumes. Things you once cared about now feel meaningless.
- **Outcome:** Unlike stress, burnout doesn't lift with a nap. It requires deeper repair—boundaries, recovery, and often professional help.

Anxiety (The Worry Stage)

- **What it is:** A heightened state of unease or dread rooted in perceived threats—whether real, imagined, or anticipated.
- **Emotions can include:** Fear, irritability, and nervousness.
- **Sounds like:** "What if something goes wrong? I can't stop thinking about it."

- **Looks like:** Restlessness, racing thoughts, stomach issues, difficulty concentrating, and hypervigilance.
- **Outcome:** Anxiety loops you into over-preparation and constant alertness. It can be managed through therapy, grounding practices, coaching, and, in some cases, medication. Left unchecked, it may escalate into panic.

Panic (The Alarm Stage)

- **What it is:** A sudden surge of intense fear or terror—that can occur without warning.
- **Emotions can include:** Terror, helplessness, and dread.
- **Sounds like:** "I'm dying. I can't breathe. Something's terribly wrong."
- **Looks like:** Rapid heart rate, chest tightness, trembling, dizziness, shortness of breath, and an overwhelming fear of losing control.
- **Outcome:** Panic attacks peak quickly (usually within ten minutes) but leave exhaustion in their wake. With grounding techniques, therapy, and sometimes medication, they can be interrupted and managed.

Meltdown (The Overflow Stage)

- **What it is:** An emotional overflow—when your system can no longer contain the buildup of tension, stress, or unprocessed feelings.
- **Emotions can include:** Rage, grief, despair, and frustration.
- **Sounds like:** "I can't take this anymore!"
- **Looks like:** Crying, yelling, lashing out, shutting down, or withdrawing. It can appear sudden to others, but inside, it feels like a cracked dam that's finally burst.
- **Outcome:** A meltdown is less about survival mode and more about release. It can bring temporary relief, but also shame or regret. Boundaries, emotional regulation, and safe outlets reduce the frequency of these behaviors.

Breakdown (The Collapse Stage)

- **What it is:** A full collapse of emotional, mental, or physical functioning after prolonged strain, trauma, or unresolved stress.
- **Emotions can include:** Depression, hopelessness, despair, and emptiness.
- **Sounds like:** "I can't do this anymore. I want to stop."
- **Looks like:** Deep exhaustion, uncontrollable crying or numbness, withdrawal from responsibilities or people, even physical illness or shutdown.
- **Outcome:** A breakdown forces urgent rest and intervention. It's a stop sign your body and mind put up when you've ignored earlier warnings. Professional support, rest, and restructuring are essential for recovery.

The Cycle Beneath the Surface

Stress ignored becomes burnout.

Burnout fuels anxiety.

Anxiety erupts into panic.

Panic loops back into stress—because now you're stressed about the panic itself.

Sometimes, overload bursts outward as a meltdown.

And if the cycle repeats long enough without recovery, the system breaks down.

In short: **Stress sparks. Burnout drains. Anxiety spirals. Panic hijacks. Meltdown spills. Breakdown collapses.** Each stage has its own voice, but together they form the cycle that quietly underpins much of our giving.

☞ **And here's the hard truth:** this cycle doesn't happen because you're weak—it happens because you've been conditioned to over-give, over-function, and over-perform. *Guarded Giving* thrives in this soil—nurtured by exhaustion and the fear of letting others down. The body may whisper through stress, scream through panic, or shut down entirely in breakdown—but underneath it all lies the same truth: unexamined motives and unchecked patterns eventually cost more than they give.

* * *

The Connection Between Ambition and Guarded Giving

Ambition and Guarded Giving share the same emotional DNA, but they express it differently. Ambition pushes you to achieve; Guarded Giving pushes you to maintain. One chases worth and validation through performance and accomplishments. The other seeks safety and worth by protecting it through service or usefulness. They look different on the surface, but both grow from the same emotional root: the fear of not being enough.

Ambition says: "If I achieve enough, I'll be valued and admired."

Guarded Giving says: "If I give enough, I'll be loved and seen."

Both wear the mask of strength and self-sufficiency. Both are fueled by anxiety, not authenticity. Both are afraid of being unseen or unworthy. And here's the truth: many of us don't realize that these patterns rarely start in adulthood. They're encouraged, modeled, and rewarded early. We are groomed to believe that being exceptional earns belonging and that being useful earns love.

Over time, we learn to equate effort with identity. Excellence becomes survival. Care becomes currency. By the time we reach adulthood, ambition and Guarded Giving have merged into a single rhythm: keep doing, keep giving, keep proving—until exhaustion feels like purpose.

The Cycle Between Ambition and Guarded Giving

It's hard to say which comes first—ambition or Guarded Giving—because they often feed each other. Ambition looks outward: it craves recognition. Guarded Giving looks inward: it craves reassurance. At first, they may seem like opposites—one self-serving, one self-sacrificing. But under the surface, both are survival strategies shaped by the same unmet need: to feel seen, valued, and safe.

Early Stage: Achievement as the Language of Love

For some, ambition comes first. You learn early that achievement equals approval—that being exceptional gets you noticed or keeps you safely unnoticed. Accomplishment becomes your love language. The better you perform, the more you're praised, protected, or at least tolerated.

But when the applause fades—or when excellence becomes the expectation instead of the exception—the emotional return starts to diminish. What once brought pride now brings pressure. The pursuit shifts from passion to preservation.

Over time, this drive to achieve turns into emotional performance—you start giving, serving, and overextending because being needed feels safer than being invisible. It's the slow transformation from achievement (external proving) to service (relational proving).

💼 The "Rich Son" – Achievement as Love Language

Think of the successful son who's achieved everything—degrees, promotions, respect—but it's still never enough for his parents. No matter how much he accomplishes, their approval remains just out of reach. As they grow older, he distances himself to protect his peace, yet he still feels obligated to take care of them. Guilt—and a conflicted mix of resignation and hope—drives his care now.

Part of him has accepted that their approval may never come; another part still wonders if love might sound different this time. That tension keeps him caught between resolution and restoration—serving from duty while quietly longing for repair. That's how ambition becomes obligation, how achievement turns into caretaking, and how the emotional pattern cycles back around.

Later Stage: When Care Becomes Currency

For others, Guarded Giving comes first. You learn to earn belonging through service—always being the dependable one, the helper, the peacemaker. Love feels conditional, tied to how much you can carry for everyone else. So you stay useful, stay available, stay needed. But as the years pass, that giving starts to cost more than it returns. Your generosity goes unreciprocated; your sacrifices unnoticed. When you finally reach your breaking point, you don't stop performing—you change the stage. You channel your care into achievement instead. You earn your worth through credentials, success, and independence. If love can't be guaranteed, at least respect can be measured.

❋ The "Devoted Daughter" – When Care Becomes Currency

Think of the devoted daughter who grew up as the family's emotional anchor—the one who managed everyone's crises, soothed tempers, and filled gaps no child should have had to fill. Her reliability became her identity. But years later, that same devotion turns to depletion. When she can no longer carry the family's burdens, she transfers that energy into professional success.

Ambition becomes her new armor—the one way she knows how to give to herself. It becomes a way to stay in control, stay impressive, stay safe. But beneath the degrees and accolades, the same fear lingers—*If I stop doing, will I still matter?* That's how service turns into striving, and how Guarded Giving transforms into ambition—the same wound, just dressed in power suits and productivity.

The Shifting Dominance of Ambition and Guarded Giving

It's not always one or the other. Most of us move between ambition and Guarded Giving depending on the season we're in. When we feel unseen, we achieve. When we feel unappreciated, we give. These patterns aren't fixed identities—they're adaptive responses. They rise and fall with our environments, our roles, and our relationships. You might lead with ambition at work and Guarded Giving at home—same wound, different expression. Recognizing which pattern you're operating from isn't about blame; it's about awareness. Because until you understand *why* you're driven, you'll keep calling depletion *"purpose"* and *"survival service."* That awareness is what makes sustainability possible.

* * *

Guarded Giving Isn't Sustainable

Faithful stewardship involves honoring your resources—your time, energy, capacity, and values—and managing them carefully, without guilt or judgment. It's not about giving less; it's about giving *wisely*.

When you're in *Guarded Giving* mode, your generosity is rooted in self-protection rather than stewardship. You're functioning from depletion—pouring from a place that's already empty. This happens when care turns into obligation, love becomes duty, and silence replaces your "no."

At this stage, you're no longer serving out of love—but out of fear: fear of letting people down, fear of being forgotten, fear of being labeled selfish. That fear hardens into resentment, and resentment becomes the emotional tax of your unspoken expectations. You're not fully disconnected—you're just trying to protect what's left. But you don't have to choose between overextending and disappearing. There's a middle ground—one rooted in clarity, not exhaustion. Stewardship lives in that middle ground. It's what happens when you give with honesty, not habit. Once you recognize your exhaustion as evidence of overextension, not failure, you've already begun setting your first boundary.

Rather than asking, "Why can't I keep up?" **Try asking:** "Why am I trying to keep up with something that drains me?" Clarity begins in that quiet pause—right after the overextension, right before the next automatic yes. It's the space where guilt meets truth, where you finally start asking not *how much* you can give, but *why* you're still giving that way. That moment is the birthplace of stewardship and the starting line of sustainability.

* * *

꩜ Emotional Arc – Chapter 1: Guarded Giving

Core Tension

"Give till it hurts"—a saying often worn like a badge of honor—can gradually damage well-being. The exhaustion of being "the one who's always there," giving without limits, and realizing that meeting others' expectations has come at the expense of self-preservation can weigh heavily on you. Consider the origins of this belief: Who first praised you for pushing past exhaustion? Who taught you that constant availability is a measure of your worth? By tracing this badge-of-honor belief to its roots, you can begin to uncover how these deeply held scripts have quietly diminished your own needs, opting instead for praise and the avoidance of disappointment.

Positive Balance

Discover that generosity becomes more powerful—and more joyful—when paired with discernment. Giving without obligation and moving toward giving with intention transform your generosity into something profound and nourishing rather than resentful and draining. When you include yourself in your care, the act of giving regains its cheerfulness and becomes sustainable.

Empowering Tone

Your stewardship isn't about how much you can endure. Instead, it's an empowering opportunity to consciously choose where your resources go. You decide to direct them to those who are either truly deserving or genuinely in need, ensuring your efforts have a lasting impact. Each thoughtful decision about where to give is an act of self-respect and a sign of your personal autonomy.

* * *

Chapter 1 Summary and Closing: Guarded Giving

You've learned to give without question—but rarely ask what it's costing you. Not all giving is generous. Sometimes it's survival disguised as selflessness. Sometimes it's silence mistaken for strength. Clarity invites awakening—an honest audit of where your energy goes and whether it's being replenished or quietly drained. Stewardship reminds you that your capacity is sacred—a finite, living resource meant to be protected, not proven. It asks you to invest your care where there is trust, alignment, and reciprocity.

From now on, you will no longer prove your worth by overextending yourself. You will protect your worth by making discerning, deliberate choices. The world will always have more needs than one person can fulfill. Your task now is to decide, with purpose, which of those needs you are *genuinely* called to address. That is where clarity becomes courage—and where generosity finally becomes sustainable.

✦ Chapter 1: Guarded Giving – Pause for Perspective

Virtue: Stewardship

Stewardship isn't just about managing resources—it's about honoring what you've been entrusted with, starting with yourself. Your time. Your energy. Your gifts. Your heart. These things are not unlimited. They are not disposable. And they are not for everyone, every time, in every way. Guarded Giving might seem noble—always showing up, always saying yes, constantly pouring out—but without discernment, it's not faithful stewardship. It's self-depletion disguised as generosity. Stewardship shifts the focus from "Who needs me?" to "Who has been entrusted with me?"

It invites reflection:

- Who has proven they can handle my trust, time, and talents with care?
- Who demonstrates mutual respect and reciprocity, not just dependence?
- Which opportunities align with my values and strengths?

In **relationships,** this means giving where there's mutual care, trust, and respect—not just need or expectation. In **your personal life,** it means treating your well-being as a non-negotiable investment, not an afterthought. In your **professional world**, stewardship means identifying goals not from ambition, but from a sense of meaning and purpose. 'It's about leveraging strategic contributions—not doing everything to prove your worth, but directing your efforts where they have the most meaningful impact. It looks like delegating wisely, setting realistic expectations, and protecting your focus so you can deliver excellence without burnout.

You cannot be an effective steward of your impact if you're careless with your source. Protecting your capacity isn't selfish—it's sacred. The better you care for your resources, the more freely you can share them in the spaces that matter most—at home, at work, and in the relationships that reflect your true calling. You've begun to see how fear, pain, and emotional exhaustion can cause you to give while disconnected from yourself—pouring from depletion instead of devotion. Now, you're invited to examine the shift: Where has your giving been an act of stewardship, and where has it been a quiet form of self-betrayal?

☞ Next Step: Workbook Journal Prompts

For a deeper reflection on how your motives for giving influence your boundaries, energy, and self-worth, refer to the companion workbook for Chapter 1.

 **Personal Notes & Insights**

Use this page to capture any quotes, ideas, or personal revelations that surfaced while reading. Let it be messy, real, and yours.

_____

_____

_____

_____

_____

_____

_____

_____

_____

_____

_____

_____

_____

_____

_____

TO THE ONE WHO THOUGHT BOUNDARIES MEANT DISAPPOINTMENT

Boundaries aren't meant to keep others out—they're about protecting yourself.

You thought boundaries would make you the bad guy. That saying "no" would sound like "I don't love you." That if you stepped back, you'd let everyone down—including the version of you who once carried it all.

So, you kept adjusting. Kept absorbing. Kept making room—even when you were crumbling inside. You didn't set boundaries because you didn't want to lose the person. You feared that safeguarding yourself might jeopardize the connection.

But clarity reveals something gentler. Something more powerful. It wasn't your boundlessness that made you a loving person. It was your devotion, your presence, and your heart. And that heart was never meant to be an open door with no rest.

Now, you're learning to set boundaries without bitterness. To honor your needs without apology. To choose solace without performance. You're learning that "no" can be sacred. That space can be an act of respect—not rejection. That silence can mean restoration—not punishment.

You're not excluding others. You're finally opening yourself up.

With clarity,
Shante

CHAPTER 2

BUILDING BOUNDARIES

Saying No Without Shame, Saying Yes Without Resentment

Every "yes" you give means saying "no" to something else. The question is: What are your yeses costing you? This chapter challenges the notion that being available, responsive, or agreeable is equivalent to being loyal, kind, or loving. You'll begin unlearning the guilt tied to saying "no" and start understanding how healthy boundaries are essential to mutual respect, emotional well-being, and self-care. Setting boundaries isn't about pushing people away; it's about showing up honestly.

But boundaries aren't just about everyone else—they're about you, too. They're about recognizing where you've been overextending *yourself* in the name of ambition, achievement, or obligation. Sometimes the boundaries we most need to set aren't with demanding people, but with unrealistic expectations, overbooked calendars, and the professional goals we set when we were running on survival mode.

Boundaries are not one-size-fits-all. The line you draw to manage everyday stress is not the same one you need when you're facing burnout, anxiety, or collapse. Many of us never learn how to scale our boundaries—we try to soothe panic with surface-level self-care or keep saying yes until our bodies intervene.

When clarity confronts the roles, rules, and silent resentments you've been carrying, the need for limits becomes undeniable. This chapter helps you understand what it means to set boundaries based on self-awareness and intention—before exhaustion sets in—and how those limits must evolve as you progress through different stages of stress and recovery.

This chapter will help you reflect on:

- What have I been afraid will happen if I start saying no?
- Whose comfort have I been protecting at the cost of my own peace?
- What goals or standards have I been chasing that no longer align with the person I'm becoming?
- What might become possible if I stopped treating exhaustion as evidence of love or loyalty?

Think of this chapter as a mirror for your motives. Boundaries are not only about what you keep out—they reveal what you've been holding in.

* * *

Proactive Versus Reactive Boundaries

Boundaries are not just principles on paper—they live in your body. You can feel the difference between a limit that's chosen with calm conviction and one that's drawn in panic. The former steadies you; the latter saves you. Both have value, but only one sustains you over time. That's where we begin: understanding the difference between boundaries built from clarity and those built from collapse.

Proactive boundary setting involves recognizing and clearly expressing your fundamental needs before they are crossed. It's rooted in self-awareness and respect.

- ☑ **Rooted**
- ☑ **Clear**
- ☑ **Intentional**
- ☑ **Sustainable**
- ☑ **Resourced**

A proactive boundary leaves you with enough energy to keep giving without depleting yourself. Reactive boundary setting, on the other hand, typically occurs after a buildup—often following pain, burnout, or betrayal.

- ⚠ **Urgent**
- ⚠ **Emotionally charged**
- ⚠ **Born from self-protection, not clarity**

The problem? Reactive boundaries can look healthy—but the motive is desperation, not discernment.

It's not: "I'm choosing peace."

It's: "I can't keep doing this."

The difference between proactive and reactive boundaries often becomes apparent in how we manage stress. If we only set limits after we're already in pain, we stay in reaction mode. But when we learn to scale our boundaries early—before depletion hits—we move from survival to stewardship.

* * *

Client Vignette: When the Breaking Point Becomes the Boundary

You met her briefly in Chapter 1—the client who logged into our first session and burst into tears before I could even finish saying hello. Once she caught her breath, the story came spilling out: her team was short-staffed, and every unfinished task somehow landed on her desk. As a leader, she felt obligated to hold it all together.

At home, her teenage son was acting out as he prepared to leave for college. She had recently finalized a divorce and was facing new health issues that drained what little energy she had left. Between work deadlines, late-night arguments, medical appointments, and constant guilt, she hadn't poured an ounce of energy back into herself in months. That first session wasn't about strategy—it was about survival. She was depleted, ashamed of her exhaustion, and afraid that resting would make her look weak.

That's when we began exploring the idea of boundaries not as walls, but as oxygen masks—tools for staying alive under pressure, not escaping it. In her case, it took a full emotional meltdown for that realization to surface. Her boundaries had always been reactive—set only after breaking points, never before them. The crisis finally forced her to pause and ask, **"Why does it take a collapse for me to care for myself?"**

If her company hadn't sponsored the coaching sessions she had with me, she probably never would have stopped long enough to ask that question at all. That's the danger of burnout culture: it rewards breakdowns disguised as dedication and treats exhaustion as evidence of loyalty. Reactive boundaries rescue you in crisis. Proactive boundaries keep you from living in one.

Reflection

- Where in your life have you waited for collapse before caring for yourself?
- What might it look like to build boundaries as an act of prevention, not recovery?

* * *

Boundaries at Every Stage

Boundaries aren't one-size-fits-all—they meet you where you are. Stress in the moment feels different from stress that persists for months, and your boundaries need to adapt to that reality. Sometimes a small reset is enough. Other times, you may need a systemic change or outside support.

Stress (Activation Stage)

- **Timeframe:** Minutes to weeks
- **What it looks like:** Headaches, restlessness, poor sleep, tension in the body.
- **Acute Stress (Minutes to Hours):** Traffic jam, presentation jitters, workplace conflict.
  - **Boundary:** In-the-moment resets. Step outside before responding. Say, "Let me get back to you in fifteen minutes." Use grounding or breathing.
  - **Clarity Statement:** "I don't have to solve this in the next five minutes."

- **Episodic Stress (Days to Weeks):** Back-to-back deadlines, family obligations, recurring conflict.
  - **Boundary:** Routine protectors. Block non-negotiable downtime. Limit after-work commitments.
  - **Clarity Statement:** "Structure is my safeguard."

- **Chronic Stress (Months to Years):** Caregiving, toxic work environments, relational tension, and financial strain.
  - **Boundary:** Systemic limits. Renegotiate workload, delegate tasks, or seek therapy or coaching.
  - **Clarity Statement:** "My body is not disposable. My limits matter."

Burnout (Depletion Stage)

- **Timeframe:** Months to years of ignored stress
- **What it looks like:** Exhaustion, cynicism, detachment, neglecting basic self-care.
- **Boundary:** Restorative limits. Take a guilt-free day (or week) off. Let others take on the tasks you usually handle. Say, "I'm not available for extras—I'm rebuilding."
- **Clarity Statement:** "Rest is not optional—I need it to' repair."

Anxiety (Worry Stage)

- **Timeframe:** Can linger indefinitely if untreated
- **What it looks like:** Racing thoughts, dread, sleeplessness, hypervigilance.
- **Boundary:** Containment. Journal worries for ten minutes, then close the book. Step away from doomscrolling. Seek professional help if needed. Tell someone, "I need reassurance, not solutions."
- **Clarity Statement:** "Fear doesn't get to run the show."

Panic (Alarm Stage)

- **Timeframe:** Peaks within about ten minutes
- **What it looks like:** Heart racing, chest tightness, fear of dying or losing control.
- **Boundary:** Safety limits. Step out of the environment. Ground yourself with breath, a calming phrase, or a familiar object. Tell yourself, "This is panic, not death. It will pass."
- **Clarity Statement:** "My body is alarmed, but I am not in danger."

Meltdown (Overflow Stage)

- **Timeframe:** Immediate spillover of unprocessed stress and emotions
- **What it looks like:** Crying, yelling, shutting down, or withdrawing.
- **Boundary:** Release. Step away and allow the emotion to surface safely. Tell someone, "I need space right now." Create a calm-down routine (music, journaling, silence).
- **Clarity Statement:** "Release is not weakness—it's relief."

Breakdown (Collapse Stage)

- **Timeframe:** After prolonged cycles of ignored stress without recovery
- **What it looks like:** Emotional, mental, or physical shutdown.
- **Boundary:** Critical intervention. Stop non-essential responsibilities. Seek professional support. Tell loved ones, "I can't do this alone—I need help now."
- **Clarity Statement:** "Survival comes first. Rebuilding can wait."

✦ **Takeaway:** Boundaries shift with time and your emotional health. Self-care regulates stress in the early phases, but once stress hardens into burnout, anxiety, or collapse, deeper limits—and sometimes professional help—become essential. These cycles don't arise out of nowhere. They're often fueled by the distorted equations we were taught about love, success, loyalty, and worth.

* * *

The Distorted Equations We've Been Fed

Availability = Loyalty → People-pleasing isn't loyalty.
Responsiveness = Love → Anxiety isn't intimacy.
Consistency = Control → Safety isn't dominance.
Silence = Rejection → Silence can be self-preservation.
Support = Sacrifice → Care doesn't require depletion.
Love = Self-Abandonment → Love doesn't demand disappearance.
Being helpful = Being lovable → Rest doesn't erase worth.
Boundaries = Rejection → Boundaries reveal respect.
Closeness = Accessibility → Intimacy honors capacity.
Presence = Care → Guilt isn't genuine care.

Reflection: Which of these reframed truths are you still wrestling to believe? Pause with the one that feels hardest to accept—it's probably the one that's been running your boundaries the longest.

⚠ *Reminder:* These truths aren't a pass to become self-centered—they're a path to balance. The goal isn't to swing to the other extreme. Clarity helps you find your middle ground—where a "yes" honors you, a "no" protects you, and a "not now" gives you room to breathe. However, to understand boundaries fully, we must step back and examine where they originated—not in human behavior, but in the intentional design that sustains all living things.

* * *

Boundaries as Design, Not Defensiveness

Before boundaries became a coaching concept, they were a biological necessity. Every living system operates within limits—cells have membranes, ecosystems have carrying capacities, and even stars burn within boundaries that sustain their light. Nature's balance depends on structure. The ocean can only reach so far up the beach without causing damage. The body can only function when its rhythms of rest and renewal are honored. The heart beats within a rhythm—it doesn't sprint endlessly, or it would fail.

The moment we try to live without limits—chasing endless productivity, availability, and control—we violate the very design that keeps us alive. Boundaries are not a restriction of life; they are the framework that makes life possible. Exhaustion isn't failure; it's feedback. It's your system's way of saying: *You've crossed your design threshold.* If every form of creation—biological, environmental, and human—depends on boundaries to thrive, why do we still treat ours like barriers instead of wisdom? Boundaries are how we live in alignment with our nature, not in opposition to it.

Just because boundaries are natural doesn't mean they come naturally. Knowing we *need* them is one thing—having the courage to enforce them is another. Design gives us the blueprint, but motivation gives us movement. Before we can honor our limits, we must understand what motivates us to protect them in the first place.

What Motivates Boundaries

Before you can set a boundary, you have to care enough to protect what's being drained. For some, that motivation is peace. For others, it's health, dignity, or the desire to stop performing endurance and start practicing self-respect. Motivation grows when you acknowledge the truth about the gap between what you need and what you continue to tolerate.

Ask yourself:

- What am I trying to preserve by staying overextended—connection, approval, safety, or control?
- What would I gain if I redirected that same energy toward restoration instead of performance?

- Am I setting boundaries out of fear of burnout or out of love for balance?

Boundaries don't start with limits—they begin with loyalty: to your design, and the version of you who deserves to live within your capacity.

* * *

What Hinders Your Motivation to Set Boundaries

Even when we know boundaries are necessary, something inside us still hesitates. Motivation doesn't just come from understanding the value of boundaries—it also grows by confronting what's blocking us from setting them.

Here are some of the most common internal and external barriers:

1. Fear of Disconnection

Many people equate boundaries with loss. You fear saying no will lead to rejection, distance, or conflict—especially if your identity has been built around being reliable or needed.

2. Guilt and Conditioning

If you were praised for selflessness or if survival required compliance, boundaries can feel like betrayal. Saying no triggers guilt because it breaks the old rule: "good people don't disappoint."

3. Unhealed Roles and Rewards

You might still be attached to the approval that came with overextending yourself. When your worth is measured by usefulness, slowing down feels like laziness rather than liberation.

4. Ambiguous Self-Image

If you don't know where you end and others begin, it's hard to know what to protect. Boundaries require self-definition and clarity about what belongs to you emotionally, mentally, and physically.

5. Performance and Perception

In leadership, family, and community roles, the desire to appear strong, capable, or "together" can override your need for restoration. You fear what protecting your peace will *look* like more than what overextending will *cost*.

6. Lack of Practice

If you've spent a lifetime accommodating others, asserting limits feels foreign, even unsafe. It's not a matter of weakness—it's just a lack of muscle memory. Boundaries are a skill, and discomfort is part of the learning curve.

Reflection:

Which of these barriers feels most familiar right now?

What story have you been telling yourself about what happens when you finally draw the line?

📖 Personal Story: When "No" Cost Me a Friendship

I once said no to a friend when she asked me to do her hair. I was exhausted, stretched thin, and didn't have the capacity. That single "no" cost me our friendship. Years of showing up for her seemed to vanish with one unmet request. It wasn't just about the friendship—her reaction echoed a message I had already internalized in countless relationships: *If I say no, they won't love me.* That's the lie many of us live by. But the truth is, it's not the boundary that erodes love; it's the absence of boundaries that drains it over time. Had I set better boundaries in the beginning of my relationship, my friend would know that she couldn't take advantage of my generosity and assume it's endless.

These patterns are fueled by the distorted equations we've inherited—beliefs that taught us to confuse depletion with devotion.

* * *

Boundaries in Context

Boundaries take different shapes depending on where they're needed. At work, they sound like, "I can meet that deadline if we adjust priorities." In leadership, they mean delegating instead of absorbing. In friendships, they mean showing up with compassion, not compulsion—being present out of care, not guilt. In marriage or partnerships, they mean saying, "I need space to process before we talk." In a family, they sound like, "I love you, but I'm not available for this conversation right now." 'In parenting, it's about teaching and modeling healthy boundaries in your own life—showing your children that self-control, humility, and discernment are not signs of weakness but marks of wisdom and honor. Because boundaries aren't just about well-being; they're about character. They're how we learn to practice modesty in desire, discipline in choice, and integrity in love.

Every setting tests a different part of who you are—your patience, your truth, your restraint. And when those boundaries are crossed, it's not only your peace that suffers—it's your principles that start to bend under pressure. When that happens, repair isn't just about confrontation; it's about correction.

Sometimes it's clarification: "Here's what I meant."

Sometimes it's a consequence: "I can't continue this way."

Sometimes it's distance: "This dynamic no longer reflects who I'm becoming."

What matters is that you move from *reaction* to *response*—from being drained by what happened to defining what happens next. Boundaries give you the courage to realign your behavior with your values and beliefs—to live within your design, not outside your dignity.

But when those limits are ignored for too long, the cost becomes internal. That's when you enter what I call **the emotional overdraft.**

* * *

The Emotional Overdraft

Sometimes, you don't slam the door—you stop answering the knock. Because every knock feels like another withdrawal on an already empty account. When you're constantly available but emotionally drained, you create an emotional overdraft—showing up out of fear, obligation, or habit while your internal balance is already in the negative.

It appears as:

- Saying yes because "who else will do it?"
- Sighing as you answer the phone.
- Being the one who constantly adjusts, always flexes, always absorbs.

It's unsustainable, and clarity confirms that. Take a breath. Think of one part of your life where this feels true—where you keep giving even though your balance is already below zero. On a scale of one to ten, how much is it costing you? Don't overthink it—the number isn't judgment, it's a flashlight. It shows you how urgent your recalibration is.

Why This Matters

Overdraft happens when we confuse depletion for growth. It takes strength to set a limit after burnout, and courage to learn to set it before burnout arrives. Both matter—but one protects you before the breaking point. When exhaustion becomes familiar, it's easy to confuse endurance with purpose. But clarity asks for a deeper kind of strength—the kind that knows when to hold on and when to let go of what love never required. Because boundary building isn't the end of giving; it's how you learn to give with limits—with wisdom, respect, and in peace.

* * *

Emotional Arc – Chapter 2: Building Boundaries

Core Tension

You've been told that showing up on demand proves loyalty. The fastest reply means the most profound love. That being "the dependable one" is a badge of honor. So you've trained yourself to be reachable, responsive, and ready—no matter the cost.

Think about the midnight work email you responded to, even though your eyes were burning. Or the text you sent back while you were supposed to be resting. Or the "Sure, I'll be there," you whispered, even when your body was screaming no. Each yes takes something from you, and the giving never stops long enough for you to recover what you've lost. You're not doubting whether to care—you're wondering if the way you've been caring is sustainable.

Positive Balance

Clarity redefines the equation: showing up doesn't mean showing up for everything. Having personal boundaries allows you to give from a place of strength rather than out of a sense of survival. They turn "always available" into "intentionally present." They create space for sharing that restores you, rather than draining you.

Empowering Tone

Every time you choose how to give rather than let guilt dictate your actions, you reclaim ownership of your time, energy, and relationships. You're no longer performing love through access; you're practicing love through connection. That choice isn't selfish; it's how you create a life where generosity and respect go hand in hand.

* * *

Chapter 2 Summary and Closing: Building Boundaries

Boundaries aren't barriers to hide behind; they are connections that facilitate genuine encounters with yourself and others. They don't diminish your love; instead, they reflect a love that endures. Clarity not only shows you where to draw the line, but also explains why that line is essential and how standing firm can safeguard the connections most meaningful to you. Every "no" you say from a place of courage makes room for a more genuine and powerful "yes." You don't need to explain your limits for them to be valid. You don't have to apologize for choosing rest over resentment. And you don't have to abandon yourself to prove your worth to anyone.

Here's the shift: Boundaries aren't the end of connection. They're the foundation of the right kind of connection. And each time you honor one, you're not just maintaining yourself; you're building a life where respect, care, and capacity can coexist without compromise.

✦ Chapter 2: Building Boundaries – Pause for Perspective

Virtue: Courage

This chapter explains how the fear of disappointing others influences your hesitation in setting boundaries. Acting with courage in boundary building means choosing to protect your energy, values, and well-being, even when it feels uncomfortable. It's about saying, "I matter enough to draw this line," and trusting that you can handle what comes next. It's not about being inflexible, but about honoring yourself without apology.

Remember: Respecting your limits preserves shared dignity. This clarity statement can act as a potent reminder to boost your confidence in the moment. It will teach others how to engage with you in healthy, sustainable ways. Teaching people how to treat us helps clarify expectations, reduce resentment, and make room for genuine connection. In relationships, courage might mean naming the unspoken, confronting disrespect, or refusing to engage in harmful dynamics.

In careers and leadership, courage in setting boundaries means standing up for your role, your time, and the well-being of your team. It can involve pushing back on unrealistic deadlines, clarifying responsibilities, or setting limits on your availability. The result? You lead with integrity, protect productivity, and demonstrate healthy work-life balance to those around you.

☞ Next Step: Workbook Journal Prompts

For a deeper reflection on how healthy boundaries can respect your needs without cutting off connection, refer to the companion workbook for Chapter 2.

 Personal Notes & Insights

Use this page to capture any quotes, ideas, or personal revelations that surfaced while reading. Let it be messy, real, and yours.

_____

_____

_____

_____

_____

_____

_____

_____

_____

_____

_____

_____

_____

_____

_____

_____

TO THE ONE WHO ALLOWED IT ALL TO BREAK SO I COULD FINALLY REBUILD

Letting go of love that demands your disappearance.

You have shown me the greatest love I've ever known—a love that met me where I was, but wouldn't coddle my disillusions. You honored me by not allowing me to stay stuck in that space. You empowered me by humbling me. You let what I built fall apart—not to punish me, but to set me free.

And now, I am rebuilding with a fresh perspective, using the blueprint you left for me. Your wisdom became my support. Your presence became my foundation. Your spirit kept me moving—even during the moments when I thought I had nothing left.

With clarity, I realize now: although broken, I was never unworthy. I didn't shatter because you held my pieces together. You waited patiently for me to see the value in those pieces. When you knew I was ready, you handed those pieces back to me—not just to rebuild, but to become someone stronger, softer, and whole.

I thank you not just for lighting my path, but for building it and trusting that I could walk it.

With clarity,
Shante

CHAPTER 3
REDEFINING LOVE

True love involves more than devotion—it calls for discernment.

If you've made it this far, you've already peeled back the layers of giving and boundary-setting. You've learned that generosity without stewardship drains you and that boundaries aren't walls—they're wisdom. Now comes the chapter that touches the core of why all of this matters in the first place: **love.**

Love is the foundation for everything that follows—how you view yourself, how you interact with others, and how you define what success truly means. It's the measure behind every motive, the thread running through every boundary and act of care. This chapter isn't a soft reflection on romance or family. It's a reckoning with the patterns we've inherited, the myths we've obeyed, and the ways we've confused **love with duty, loyalty with silence, and endurance with acceptance.**

You've started building boundaries; now it's time to see what they're protecting. You've examined your giving; now it's time to expand your understanding of why and how to give from a place of love. This is where clarity meets compassion—where you begin to ask whether the way you love still aligns with the truth you've started to see.

Love, Boundaries, and Balance

Let's be clear: this chapter does not argue against sacrifice. True love does require endurance, patience, forgiveness, and, yes, self-sacrifice. The aim here is not to teach you to love less but to love wisely. To love others without losing the ability to love yourself. It's not about abandoning people or relationships the moment they require effort. You don't have to cut ties with people who can't meet every need. It's about **not sacrificing your dignity and peace of mind in the hope of being loved.**

What we seek is balance—not burnout. Love that honors both grace and wisdom. Love that incorporates self-care, mutuality, and self-respect. Genuine love creates space for both truth and tenderness. It doesn't use honesty as a weapon or confuse bluntness with bravery. Real love considers delivery as much as it values truth. It speaks from care, not ego. You can tell the truth without tearing someone down. You can set a boundary without belittling. You can be honest without humiliating.

True love isn't cruel or careless—it's clear. It's not passive, but it's never punitive. It may require courage and uncomfortable conversations, but it never sacrifices kindness for the sake of truth, nor does it bury truth for the sake of peace. Love that silences honesty isn't safe. And love that prides itself on "just being real" while indulging in self-righteous condemnation isn't love—it's ego dressed as virtue.

Real love embodies both clarity and compassion, boundaries and benevolence, truth and tact. It seeks to build, not bruise—to correct without control, to express without harm, and to connect without diminishing anyone involved.

How does your definition of love shape how you show up in life? And what would shift if you began to practice love as both a personal and professional principle?

* * *

The Four Types of Love

Even science can't quite agree on what love actually is. Psychologists, philosophers, and theologians have tried to define it for centuries—some calling it an emotion, others a virtue, or even a deliberate practice. But what's clear is that not all love is the same. Understanding the different types of love helps you discern whether what you're giving—or receiving—is rooted in principle, emotion, or expectation.

The ancient Greeks described love in four key expressions: **storge, philia, eros, and agape.** These distinctions are timeless because they help us understand not just who we love—but *how*.

Storge – Family Love

Storge is the natural affection between family members, the kind that grows from familiarity, responsibility, and shared history. It appears when a parent sacrifices sleep for a newborn or when siblings protect each other, even when they spend most of their time arguing. But for those raised in trauma, love and loyalty often become tangled with fear and performance, creating patterns where affection feels conditional and unsafe. Over time, storge can become strained when duty replaces genuine connection or when care becomes compensation for chaos.

Philia – Friendship Love

Philia is warm, chosen love—the loyalty between friends who truly see and support each other. It's the laughter that makes hard days bearable, the confidant who keeps your truths safe. This kind of love grows between people who share values, not just interests. It flourishes through mutual respect and emotional safety.

Eros – Romantic Love

Eros is passionate love, charged with attraction and desire. It's the spark that draws people together—the chemistry that can inspire both intimacy and illusion. When balanced by respect and honesty, eros deepens connection; when left unchecked, it can blur boundaries and disguise control as devotion or abuse as passion.

Agape – Principled Love

Agape is the highest form of love—unselfish, moral, and deliberate. It's love guided by principle rather than impulse or sentiment. It's the choice to show care even when it's inconvenient, to act with integrity even when emotions run high. Agape shows up when a leader advocates for their team's well-being, when a parent lovingly disciplines, or when you extend grace to yourself after falling short. This kind of love isn't' blind; it's anchored.

Each form of love serves a purpose. The challenge is knowing which one you're operating from—and whether it aligns with your values. Because love without discernment becomes chaos. But love rooted in wisdom becomes strength.

* * *

The Wisdom to Love Well

In striving to express love in an unselfish, principled way, wisdom must walk hand in hand with compassion. Even the purest motives can become distorted when love isn't balanced with discernment. You can care so deeply that you forget to come up for air—so devoted to doing good that you quietly self-destruct. Real love does not require collapse to prove its sincerity.

True, unselfish love requires knowledge, humility, and divine wisdom for its proper expression. It must be guided by principles that are already true and established—not ones invented to excuse harm or justify comfort. These principles echo across faith, psychology, and moral philosophy:

- **Reciprocity:** Healthy love is mutual. It respects give-and-take, not constant depletion.
- **Integrity:** Love and deception cannot coexist; truth-telling is a form of care.
- **Stewardship:** We are responsible for what we nurture—including our energy, relationships, and peace.
- **Respect for free will:** Love never forces or manipulates; it allows choice and honors boundaries.
- **Accountability:** Real love includes responsibility—for words, actions, and their impact.
- **Humility:** Love doesn't seek superiority; it seeks understanding.

These are not subjective preferences; they are enduring truths that remain constant even as culture shifts. Love without these universally accepted truths becomes sentiment without structure. And just as we saw in Chapter 1, giving without clarity can become performance. Real love gives from integrity, not impulse—because love and giving are inseparable acts of stewardship.

Love, when aligned with wisdom, gives from integrity—not obligation. Each of the four facets—**eros, storge, philia, and agape**—has the potential to create profound peace and joy. But only when that love is anchored in enduring standards.

* * *

The Illusion of Unconditional Love

Now that we've explored the different forms of love and how they appear across our relationships, it's time to address one of the most misunderstood concepts of all: **unconditional love.**

Television, movies, music, and even well-meaning family and friends have romanticized a version of love that knows no limits and demands no accountability—even when it destroys peace. This version of love is often praised as noble, but in reality, it's dangerous. When we admire love that requires nothing in return—no honesty, growth, or responsibility—we begin to equate **low self-worth with low maintenance.** We celebrate depletion as devotion. We confuse being chosen with being cherished.

This distortion leads many to mistake acceptance of mistreatment as a badge of honor and silence for forbearance. But true love isn't the absence of limits—it's the presence of integrity. Because when you love without boundaries, you don't just lose yourself; you lose the structure that gives love meaning.

And so, many of us move through life starved for genuine connection yet burdened by the cost of misaligned relationships. What often feels like love is sometimes loyalty to dysfunction—where care turns into compliance and closeness becomes control. Before we can free ourselves from that cycle, we have to understand the difference between enduring love with strength and accepting pain as normal. The difference between the two determines whether love refines you or erases you.

Endurance Versus Acceptance

Endurance and acceptance are often confused, especially in relationships that emphasize unconditional love. But they are not the same.

Acceptance, when distorted by "struggle love," convinces you that pain is proof of devotion. It whispers, "This is just how love is." It numbs your discernment, quiets your resistance, and keeps you compliant under the guise of commitment. In this state, acceptance becomes the anesthetic of self-betrayal—keeping you still in situations that require movement.

Endurance is different. It's not silence; it's strategy. It's the quiet strength that allows you to withstand what you can't immediately change *without letting it change you.* Endurance doesn't mean you approve of the pain—it means you're surviving it with your sanity intact while gathering the clarity, courage, and circumstances needed to create change.

Acceptance, in this context, surrenders your power.

Endurance preserves it.

While both may look the same from the outside, since both involve staying, only one keeps your soul awake.

Endurance says, "I will not let this break me."

Acceptance says, "Maybe I was meant to be broken."

The difference is crucial. One leads to healing; the other to hiding. The true essence of endurance doesn't bind you to pain—it buys you time to see clearly. Used wisely, it can help you build the qualities you'll need later—the strength, patience, and discernment to manage what life may bring next. It's the quiet grace that keeps you grounded until the lesson has finished, teaching what it came to teach. And when that clarity arrives, endurance must evolve into discernment. Because strength without wisdom can keep you in places that clarity is trying to release you from.

The moment you stop accepting survival mode as the status quo is when endurance begins its actual work. It's the quality that allows you to hold onto self-respect, dignity, and worth—even when others try to diminish them. And although your circumstances may not change immediately, endurance changes *you.*

Conditional Versus Unconditional Love

It's important to note that the opposite of unhealthy *unconditional* love isn't *conditional* love. Conditional love says, "I'll care for you as long as you meet my expectations." It withholds affection until you perform, comply, or please. That kind of love is not care, it's control. Healthy love doesn't swing between extremes—it's guided by principle. It neither demands perfection to earn connection nor tolerates harm to preserve it. Real love is accountable and mutual. It sets boundaries without withholding affection, and it offers mercy without abandoning truth.

Letting Go of the Illusion

We were taught that love endures—that real love holds on, keeps giving, and proves its depth through perseverance. But no one told us that closeness without care breeds resentment, or that presence without peace erodes intimacy. When someone repeatedly drains your energy, breaks trust, or demands that you stretch beyond your capacity to keep the relationship alive, it is emotional exploitation.

Letting go doesn't mean the love is gone; it means you finally saw the pattern clearly—the same one that required your silence, your sacrifice, and your unreciprocated loyalty. With clarity, you realize you can mourn what you hoped love would become while honoring the wisdom that tells you it can't grow in dishonor. This is one of the unspoken costs of clarity—the grief that comes when you choose peace over proximity. It's the heartbreak of knowing you still care, but can no longer carry the connection alone.

Sometimes, you're not just mourning the relationship—you're grieving the version of yourself who believed that if you loved enough, they would change. You're grieving the story you built around potential. But that version didn't die; it never truly lived. And clarity asks you to release it—not because love failed, but because illusion did. Even when we begin to understand what genuine love requires, letting go of the counterfeit version still hurts. But that pain is sacred. It means your heart is finally learning how to distinguish between them. After illusion comes truth. And with truth comes the invitation to unlearn everything you were taught about what love is supposed to be.

* * *

Myths About True Love

Once you begin to see the difference between illusion and truth, the myths you were taught about love start to unravel. Some were meant to protect you. Others were meant to control you. Either way, they shaped how you give, receive, and define love—and now, it's time to challenge them. Because once clarity opens your eyes, it becomes harder and harder to pretend. Let's directly call out some of those love myths:

✗ Unlimited Availability = Love

You were taught that real love means constantly being accessible and always showing up. But love that demands constant access without considering your capacity is not care—it's consumption.

☑ Intentional Connection = Love

Real love values your time, energy, and presence. It cherishes quality over quantity, opting for meaningful moments of connection over constant performance.

✗ Self-Erasure = Love

You learned that love meant shrinking yourself to keep the peace. That isn't compromise—it's self-abandonment.

☑ **Mutual Regard = Love**

True love respects your voice, not just your role. It honors individuality, not invisibility. Love should never require you to silence your own truth to preserve someone else's comfort.

✗ **Enduring Mistreatment = Love**

You were told that to love deeply means to suffer quietly. But suffering silently isn't love—it's survival mode disguised as loyalty.

☑ **Safe Reciprocity = Love**

Real love can be challenging, but it is never harmful. It is grounded in mutual care and shared responsibility, where both people take ownership of the emotional environment they create together.

✗ **Performing = Love**

You believed that love had to be earned through achievements, helpfulness, or perfection. But performance-based love always leaves you chasing approval instead of receiving affection.

☑ **Being Valued for Your Whole Self = Love**

Real love doesn't require auditions. It invites authenticity. It creates space for growth, imperfection, and truth, choosing connection over appearance.

✗ **Misguided devotion = Love.**

You accepted what caused you pain and called it commitment—devotion without discernment becomes destruction.

☑ **Rooted Commitment = Love**

Healthy love honors both boundaries and bonds. 'It isn't sustained by guilt or fear.

Relationships are nuanced, so for a moment, shift the focus from *the person* to *the pattern*. Ask yourself: Which of these false forms of love have I mistaken for connection? And what would change if I began to align my love with truth rather than tolerance?

🚨 **If you're in a situation involving emotional, physical, psychological, financial, or spiritual abuse—please know you deserve safety and support. Seek out help immediately.**

Closing Reflection on Illusion

Many of us were taught to see love as purely a feeling—a condition of the heart. But true love is also a discipline. It is guided by moral wisdom, understanding, and discernment, not just emotion. Real love takes into account both intention and impact. It's not about loving harder—it's about loving wiser.

And when clarity arrives, it often carries disillusionment in its hands—the grief, shock, and loss of innocence. The quiet ache that comes from seeing clearly what you once idealized. Disillusionment isn't cynicism; it's what remains when fantasy fades and truth takes its rightful place. Only when the illusion breaks can authentic love begin to build. Sometimes, the breaking is what finally teaches you what love was never meant to cost.

* * *

The High Price of Misaligned Love

Dismissive comments. One-sided effort. Expectations that only seemed to flow one way. No apologies. Promises broken like clockwork. You believed that true love meant holding on—no matter how heavy it became. So, you kept trying to make the connection work. Not because it felt good, but because it felt familiar. Because when it was good, it was *almost* enough. You stayed because they had good intentions. Because no one ever asked you the question that finally stopped you in your tracks:

Is this love supporting me—or slowly breaking me?

We don't just struggle in relationships because of *who* we love—we struggle because of *how* we've been taught to love, and what we've been taught to accept as love. When your idea of love is shaped by pain, performance, or proximity, it distorts your sense of self-worth. You start to confuse control with care, attachment with intimacy, and loyalty with self-erasure.

Trauma Bonding

Research in trauma bonding, attachment theory, and family systems has long shown this pattern: When your early experiences of love involved volatility, inconsistency, or emotional labor beyond your years, your nervous system learns to equate love with work—and safety with survival. So you push yourself past your limits, hoping that "loving harder" will finally create security. But love that costs you your dignity or identity is too expensive.

Take a Moment:

- Reflect on how big-hearted people often attract **takers— not givers**, because their kindness is viewed as a weakness to exploit.

- Reflect on how **distorted love**—characterized by inconsistency, control, or emotional confusion—can cloud your judgment, blur your boundaries, and slow your healing.
- Reflect on how **over-functioning** alters expectations, makes emotional labor seem like love, and teaches you to accept what should never be considered normal.

A Familiar Pattern

Clarifying the Context: Before we go further, it's essential to understand that what follows applies to relationships in which both people have the capacity—and the willingness—to grow. The patterns described here exist in functional but misaligned relationships, not in abusive or coercive ones. In trauma-bonded dynamics, "working it out" often deepens harm rather than resolves it. Real healing in those cases begins with safety, not strategy—with distance, not dialogue.

Across dozens of my clients, friends, and family members, I've seen the same story repeat itself: women who are married with children quietly carry everything. At the same time, their husbands drift in and out of emotional presence. The bills, the schedules, the children, the invisible labor—all of it rests on their shoulders. There's no proof of betrayal, but the absence feels just as sharp. Many describe it as feeling like "a single married woman"—bound by vows but left to carry the weight alone.

The breaking point usually comes when they realize that what they've been calling love is actually survival: enduring neglect and hoping his presence will finally match their efforts.

But men carry patterns too—different, yet equally costly.

Many were taught that love is proven through protection, provision, and endurance—that showing emotion makes them weak or unreliable. So they love through doing, not expressing. They give in the ways they were told a "good man" should. But over time, some find that their worth is measured only by what they provide, not by who they are. Their consistency becomes expected rather than appreciated. Their efforts become invisible, and their silence is mistaken for indifference. Meanwhile, they watch the woman they love grow increasingly dissatisfied.

Their breaking point often arrives quietly—when they realize that despite giving everything materially, they still feel unseen, misunderstood, and unloved. Because no matter how capable they appear, no one has truly seen the man behind the role.

What both patterns share isn't blame—it's imbalance.

Two people trying to love within the limits of what they were taught. One overextending to feel valued; the other overperforming to feel respected. Both mistaking survival patterns for connection, and both deserving of a love that allows them to be fully human—seen, safe, and supported. When patterns of misaligned love repeat over generations, they cease to appear as dysfunction and begin to seem like tradition. They're passed down in stories, vows, and songs—repackaged as strength. But beneath the surface, they all share the same core distortion: the belief that love must hurt to be real. That belief manifests differently in every culture, but the ache of the storyline remains the same.

* * *

Struggle Love, by Any Name

"Struggle love" is a term widely recognized in the Black community. It's used to describe relationships built on tolerating hardship, proving loyalty through pain, and mistaking suffering for depth and intimacy. Yet across many generations, struggle love has been passed down as a blueprint for devotion: the idea that the more chaos you survive, the more deserving you are of being chosen. But struggle love isn't just generational; it's also cultural, wearing different names across communities:

- In Caucasian families, it might be called codependency, staying together for the kids—martyrdom worn as a badge of honor.
- In Latinx households, it is often wrapped in romanticism—*amor con sacrificio*—blending love and suffering as a virtue and proof of loyalty.
- In Asian cultures, it may manifest as duty-bound silence: staying, serving, and suppressing—for the sake of harmony, reputation, and survival.

Before we proceed, let's be clear: the "struggle" described here isn't the natural tension or perseverance that healthy, long-term relationships require as they navigate life's uncertainties and pain. It refers to something much heavier—the intentional or repeated mistreatment, neglect, or emotional manipulation that one person inflicts and the other tolerates in the name of love. That kind of struggle is not love; it's survival.

Whether shaped by culture, religion, or tradition, the message remains: the more you suffer, the more your love is validated. But love that demands your depletion is conditioning. No matter the culture or the legacy—if what you know as love leaves you empty, erases you, or makes you doubt your worth, it's an inherited mindset that confuses pain with purpose—and it's costing you.

The Scripts We Inherited

The script varies, but the message stays the same: prove your worth through pain and call it passion. "Ride or die" love means being loyal through betrayal now, so that you will be chosen later. Staying, even when you're unseen, unheard, or undone, is celebrated as the ultimate act of devotion. Holding someone down while they repeatedly let you down is framed as faithfulness, not foolishness.

And this isn't just folklore—it's in our soundtracks. Songs like **Beyoncé's "Love on Top"** have been played at countless weddings, including my own. But beneath the melody lies the message we've been fed for generations: glorify tolerance and accept struggle as part of the love story.

This isn't the kind of love we *endure*; it's the kind we *choose*, often without realizing it. Because we've been conditioned to believe that the wait, the tears, and the "almosts" make the eventual payoff meaningful. We've danced to these messages, toasted to them, and even built vows around them.

But that's not intimacy—it's a trauma economy. It trains you to earn connection through exhaustion and to mistake inconsistency for care. And if love finally shows up after all the struggle, the story gets rewritten as redemption: "See? It was worth it."

It wasn't. **Struggle love isn't noble—it's manipulative.** Love that demands your depletion isn't love—it's conditioning. It pairs two opposing forces that were never meant to coexist. "Struggle love" is, by definition, an oxymoron. Struggle implies conflict, confusion, and survival; love is meant to provide safety and connection. One depletes. The other restores. You can't chain yourself to something that drains you and still call it love. It's emotional exploitation disguised as culture, romance, or religion. The good news? Legacies like this don't have to be repeated—they can be rewritten.

✦ **"If love feels like a battlefield, it's not love—it's psychological training for emotional warfare."**

* * *

What Aligned Love *Actually* Is

Aligned love is based on principles. It moves with compassion and clarity. It may challenge you, but it won't break you. It may require patience, but never at the expense of unconditional acceptance or sacrificing your integrity or beliefs. And here's the quiet beauty of aligned love: when everyone prioritizes respecting the other's well-being, no one ends up empty. Love then becomes the overflow—not the sacrifice.

The Quiet Test of Love

Boundaries are not walls—they are mirrors. They reveal who's willing to meet you in truth and who only loves you when it's convenient. They separate genuine connection from conditional care. True love doesn't ask you to disappear to keep the peace. It invites you to stay honest, even when honesty changes everything.

Love or Labor?

Loving someone is one thing. Working to earn the right to be loved is another. Ask yourself:

- *Have I confused peacekeeping with peace?*
- *Do I give more than I genuinely have to offer?*
- *Do I feel safe being transparent—or am I only tolerated when I'm agreeable?*

You can love deeply without losing yourself. You can mourn what was possible while accepting what is real. Because love that demands silence for survival is not love—it's labor. And the work of proving your worth will always cost more than it gives back.

When love feels heavy, instead of asking, "Why am I so hard to love?" ask, "Why do I keep calling it love when it asks me to shrink?" and "What would love look like if it didn't require my disappearance?"

You're not asking for too much. You're seeking a genuine connection. Let's redefine what love means—so it no longer comes at the expense of who you are.

*　*　*

✍ Emotional Arc – Chapter 3: Redefining Love

Core Tension

The main struggle we examined in this chapter is the clash between what we were taught love should be and what healthy love actually is. You began this chapter still carrying inherited ideas of love rooted in tolerance, performance, and self-depletion—believing that giving endlessly, even at your own expense, made you worthy of being loved. The discomfort comes from realizing that much of what you've called love was, in fact, survival—hidden beneath cultural conditioning, family scripts, or unspoken expectations. This awareness brings with it grief, guilt, and even a temporary loss of identity. Because redefining love often requires unlearning the very scripts that once shaped how you've connected with others your entire life.

Positive Balance

Clarity doesn't always arrive with comfort—it often comes with the ache of disillusionment. But that ache means you're no longer chained to the falsehoods that once defined you. Redefining love also gives you the power to redefine success—not as constant striving or an endless pattern of self-sacrifice, but as alignment. Success now looks like peace that doesn't require performance, connection that doesn't demand compliance, and love that doesn't require loss. You now understand that love and self-respect can—and should—coexist. You may still wrestle with remnants of the old illusion, but it no longer rules you. You can see the truth, even if you're still learning how to live it.

Empowering Tone

Every time you choose to love with discernment rather than rely on old patterns, you create space for a connection that strengthens rather than depletes you. You're no longer proving your worth through suffering—you're practicing love through honesty, grace, and mutual respect. That choice isn't abandonment—it's alignment. And it's how you build relationships that feel like peace, not punishment.

* * *

Chapter 3 Summary and Closing: Redefining Love

Love isn't the absence of conflict, sacrifice, or discomfort. Instead, it's the presence of principles, peace, and mutual respect. Many of us have been taught to prove our love by tolerating pain, pushing ourselves harder, and erasing parts of ourselves to keep the connection alive. True love doesn't punish your boundaries or make your exhaustion a requirement for connection. Clarity encourages you to redefine what love truly means—not just as a transaction, but as a transformative alignment. Love without discernment turns into enabling. Loyalty without reciprocity becomes self-betrayal. And connection without care turns into chaos.

You can remain loving while walking away. You can grieve and still grow. This chapter isn't about abandoning others—it's about no longer abandoning yourself. It focuses on recognizing and releasing patterns that cloud your clarity. The simple truth is: Love does not weaken you; it empowers you. You have the right to seek love that brings peace, not punishment.

✨ Chapter 3: Redefining Love – Pause for Perspective

Virtue: Discernment

Discernment guides you in distinguishing between care and control, connection and co-dependency, and love and emotional labor. It's not only about how others love you; it also shapes how you love yourself and what you choose to reciprocate in how you love others. Are your actions driven by genuine alignment or quiet obligation? Do you uphold your standards or slowly weaken them for the sake of harmony?

Discernment invites you to love wisely rather than out of fatigue—to offer support that is sustainable, not self-destructive. In relationships, it's the honesty to see when love is mutual and principled—and when it's one-sided or enabling. It's the courage to respect others' standards while expecting yours to be honored. It asks you to take responsibility—not just inventory—and to connect without trying to control. The most powerful love isn't only tender—it's transparent in what it gives, what it can't give, and what it allows. It's love expressed from strength, not weakness—from clarity, not fear.

At work, discernment determines how you allocate your time, trust, and energy. 'It's about being aware of when to give more, when to pause, and when to walk away completely. Leaders who practice discernment protect their teams' well-being without sacrificing integrity. They avoid *struggle leadership* the same way they avoid *struggle love*—by ensuring that professional relationships are built on respect, reciprocity, and truth rather than constant sacrifice.

reflect on the unhealthy ways you've defined love in your life—and what needs to be released or realigned.

☞ Next Steps: Workbook Journal Prompts

For a deeper look at how discernment impacts your ability to express and receive love, refer to the companion workbook for Chapter 3.

 Personal Notes & Insights

Use this page to capture any quotes, ideas, or personal revelations that surfaced while reading. Let it be messy, real, and yours.

_____

_____

_____

_____

_____

_____

_____

_____

_____

_____

_____

_____

_____

_____

TO THE ONE WHO SAW ME BEFORE I SAW MYSELF

Rediscover your dignity without settling.

You saw me long before I ever knew how to see myself. You saw the pain behind my ambition—the self-betrayal behind my sacrifice. You knew my heart was sincere, but I lacked maturity in my judgment. You knew the goals I set were meant to fill a void. You knew I gave too much to those who broke my trust, mistaking closeness for purpose. You knew I was confused about the difference between being trusted and being known.

But you? You recognized my limits and still called me worthy. You saw my patterns and still reached out again and again. You saw not only who I was, but also who I could become. You never required perfection—only progress, presence, and honesty. With clarity, I now understand: Self-sacrifice is only sacred when it's offered freely. Not out of guilt, fear, a desire for acceptance, or to avoid rejection. It must come without hypocrisy, without resentment, and never at the expense of self-respect.

Now, I honor my limitations, not just as flaws to be fixed—but as a divine reminder of where grace meets me. Thank you for seeing all of me—even when I was at my lowest. Even when I was giving love, I didn't know how to give to myself. You saw me, and because of that, I am learning to see myself more clearly, too.

With clarity,
Shante

CHAPTER 4
RESPECT AND SELF-BETRAYAL

Begin by honoring yourself—and observe how respect naturally follows.

Chapter 4 explores respect and betrayal—not just as abstract concepts, but as genuine experiences that shape the self, the family, and society as a whole. This chapter invites you to explore what genuine respect looks like in daily life—including at work, at home, and within yourself. It examines how clarity fosters self-respect and how confusion often leads to self-betrayal. It promotes a view of respect that allows for both humility and courage, as well as accountability and advocacy.

It affirms that genuine respect and humility don't mean staying silent or pulling back—they mean knowing when to speak up, stand firm, and show up with purpose. Clarity isn't disrespectful. Reinforcing your boundaries isn't arrogance. If either is missing, even your best intentions can lead to chaos inside and out. You can honor others without dishonoring yourself. You can't be in the habit of dishonoring others and still consider yourself honorable.

Loving from Strength

Clarity may have taught you what love is not, but respect teaches you how to love well. After shedding the illusions of unconditional love, this next step is about learning to love from a place of strength—where your care no longer costs you your clarity. Respect is what transforms emotional awareness into emotional maturity; it's where love becomes accountable.

Loving from strength means you love from wholeness, not from hunger. It's choosing to love because you want to, not because you need to. It's rooted in discernment, boundaries, and emotional maturity—where love becomes an overflow of inner peace, not a desperate attempt to earn it. When you love from strength:

- You give freely, but not foolishly.
- You stay compassionate without becoming consumed.
- You choose connections that honor your dignity.
- You understand that love is an act of stewardship, not self-erasure.

Loving from weakness, by contrast, comes from fear, dependency, manipulation, or identity confusion.

- It's love motivated by anxiety—"If I stop giving, they'll leave."
- It seeks safety through compliance instead of clarity.
- It gives affection to avoid rejection, not to build a connection.
- It is love that is performed to prove worth.

💬 Vignette: The Moment of Realization

During one of my past relationships, I began to sense that something beneath the surface wasn't right. On the outside, the relationship looked healthy—steady, gentle words, constant agreement, no visible conflict—but something in me felt uneasy. Every conversation ended with, "Whatever you want." Every decision deferred to me. It should have felt honoring, but it didn't. It felt staged.

I remember confiding in my best friend: "This isn't what it's supposed to be." She replied, "Oh, but I can tell he loves you." My immediate response became one of the most defining statements of my life. I replied: "I want someone to love me from a place of strength, not from a place of weakness." I didn't even know at the time the depths of my desire. What I was really saying was:

"I want to be met, not mirrored."

"I don't need agreement; I need authenticity."

"I'd rather face some healthy tension than live in a lie."

Loving from strength is when both people bring their whole selves to the relationship—opinions, imperfections, individuality, and all—and still choose each other from that place of authenticity. I wasn't rejecting love; I was rejecting counterfeit connection. The so-called love I had received was really performance and appeasement. He had no clear self to give me.

That experience taught me something sacred: love offered from a fractured self can never sustain real intimacy. When love lacks authenticity, it turns into control—either controlling **how the other person sees you** or **controlling the space so truth remains suppressed.** To love from strength, both people must be grounded in who they are. This is what allows respect to become the hinge—the moment love shifts from illusion to integrity.

When respect becomes the hinge, love can finally move the way it's meant to—able to open and close in balance. Without it, love loses structure. It either locks (control, fear, illusion) or swings wildly (chaos, overgiving, self-betrayal). But when respect enters the picture—when both people honor boundaries, individuality, and truth—love gains integrity. It becomes steady, sustainable, and honest. Strength-based love respects individuality; it doesn't mimic or minimize it. It recognizes that genuine respect isn't compliance—it's coexistence.

* * *

What Are Respect and Self-Respect?

Respect goes beyond politeness. It's more than just being liked or admired. It is the active recognition of someone's worth, which requires understanding what motivates or moves them, and using that knowledge to treat them with love that protects, honors, and affirms that value. It's how you show someone they matter. It's how you protect what's sacred. It's how you communicate, "You are safe to be yourself here."

And here's the crucial part: **respect isn't a prize to be earned—it's the baseline you're owed.** You don't have to "prove" your worth to be treated with dignity. Trust may take time. Intimacy may require reciprocity. But respect? Respect is the floor, not the ceiling.

Respect in Action

Respect sounds like: invitations to speak, lingering questions, and gestures that say, "Your voice matters."

Respect looks like: honoring boundaries, valuing time, and acknowledging contributions without caveats.

Why It's Not Passivity:

Respect isn't silence—it's strength under control. It doesn't retreat; it responds with intention. It's knowing when to stay silent and when to stand firm without losing your voice.

Turning It Inward:

The same principle applies to how you treat yourself. Self-respect is internalized respect—your daily practice of honoring your limits, values, and voice. When you stop abandoning yourself for approval, you stop silencing your own needs, truths, and instincts to keep others comfortable. You call that silence "peace," but the calmness isn't because things are resolved—it's calm because you've avoided the conflict by muting yourself. Respect—both given and received—creates the foundation for clarity. Together with dignity, self-worth, and self-esteem, it keeps your internal system aligned—like the parts of a car moving in sync.

Think of it this way: Your inner world runs like a vehicle. Each part—dignity, worth, respect, and esteem—has a role in how smoothly you move through life. When one part falters, the whole system feels it. But when they work together, you move with balance, direction, and peace.

* * *

The Self in Motion: Car Metaphor Framework

Dignity = The VIN Number

Every car has a unique VIN engraved into it as soon as it is made. This number doesn't disappear or change if the paint chips or the engine breaks down. Similarly, every human being is marked with inherent worth. You may feel damaged or changed by experiences, but your existence means you are valuable.

→ **Dignity** is the foundation that shows every person is valued from the beginning.

Humanity = The Drive

A car isn't meant to stay polished in a garage—its purpose is to be driven. Our humanity is what turns dignity into connection. Without it, worth becomes abstract. Humanity reminds us that behind every "label" is a living person with emotions and a story.

→ **Humanity** serves as the bridge that makes dignity relational, not merely abstract. It's our shared ability to connect and respect one another.

Self-Worth = The Fuel

Without fuel, the car can't move. Self-worth is the inner conviction: **"I matter because I exist."** Unlike dignity—which is permanent and given by design—self-worth reflects how much of that dignity you've claimed. It's not about whether you *are* valuable; it's about whether you believe it. It rises and falls with how you treat yourself, the choices you make, and the boundaries you set. If you don't nurture your self-worth, you end up waiting for someone else to give you fuel to keep you going.

→ **Self-worth** drives your ability to advance with purpose.

Respect = The Turn Signals

Turn signals indicate to others where you're headed. Respect functions similarly—it shows your direction and boundaries. When you use your "signal," you're communicating: Here's who I am, here's what I value, and here's how I expect to be treated. This clarity helps prevent confusion and lowers the risk of collisions. But here's the key: **you don't need to earn the right to use your signal.** Every driver on the road has that courtesy. Likewise, every person deserves basic respect—dignity, honesty, and care. Others may not always agree with your direction, but at least they can see which way you intend to go.

→ **Respect** is about communication, not control.

Self-Respect = The Steering Wheel

The steering wheel guides your direction. Self-respect is a daily choice to stay true to your core values. With it, you maintain your integrity instead of letting others' expectations lead you astray. It helps you avoid drifting into people-pleasing or tolerating mistreatment.

→ Respect for others is a responsibility. **Self-respect** is a choice.

Sidebar: Self-Respect = Living Your Core Values: When you act in line with your core values, you strengthen your dignity and uphold your worth.

✯ Reflection Prompt: Core Values Check-In

Think of your core values as the road signs that keep your steering steady. Name three values that define how you move through life. Then ask yourself: *Where have my recent choices drifted from them—and what minor adjustment can help me realign?*

Self-Esteem = The GPS

The GPS shows you how you're doing on the road. Like the reliability of a GPS unit, self-esteem fluctuates in response to circumstances. One day, the signal is strong and clear, the next day, it's fuzzy or off track. That's because self-esteem reflects how you feel about yourself at the moment—it's influenced by performance, feedback, and context. If you only depend on it, you'll always feel like you're recalibrating after every wrong turn. When rooted in dignity, worth, and respect, self-esteem becomes a guide instead of a verdict. Detours don't diminish your value—they're just part of the journey.

→ **Self-esteem** drives progress, but it isn't the basis of your worth.

Sidebar: Capacity = The Fuel Tank: Your tank doesn't alter the quality of the fuel—it only determines how much it can hold. Capacity measures how much you can carry in a given season—emotionally, spiritually, physically, and mentally. Overfill it, and you burn out. Respect it, and you make a sustainable impact and progress.

→ **Capacity** is your limit, not your flaw.

How These Pieces Work Together

Aspect	Self-Respect	Self-Worth	Self-Esteem
Based on	Values & standards	Inherent human dignity	Performance & feedback
Stability	Steady & grounded	Rooted and constant	Fluctuates with wins & losses
Purpose	Guards your dignity	Affirms your worth	Guides growth and reflection
Main Question	"What will I allow?"	"Am I worthy?"	"How am I doing?"

When dignity, worth, and respect stay aligned, self-betrayal is nearly impossible. But when even one of them breaks down, the system starts to falter—and betrayal, whether from others or from within, enters the picture.

* * *

💬 **Client Reflection:**

"It wasn't one big betrayal," she said. "It was a thousand small moments when I kept letting things slide—when I told myself it wasn't worth the argument."

What is Betrayal?

This is how many betrayals begin: quietly, under the banner of keeping the peace. Betrayal is simple at its core—it's the breaking of trust, safety, and sincerity—the fracture between what was promised and what was delivered. Betrayal wears many faces. Sometimes it's loud—like infidelity. Sometimes it's quiet—like being constantly dismissed or unseen. Sometimes it's emotional neglect that leaves you invisible. Sometimes it's deception that leaves you doubting your own perception. But all forms share a common root: the erosion of trust and safety. And the most challenging part? It rarely comes from strangers. It comes from the people who were supposed to love you, protect you, and stand beside you. Below are some of the most common ways betrayal appears—especially in family systems, where the wounds tend to echo the longest.

Betrayals of Connection

These betrayals rupture emotional safety—the foundation of healthy love and respect. These moments teach you that love and danger can coexist.

Emotional Betrayal: Ignoring, mocking, or minimizing someone's feelings. Showing up to celebrate success but disappearing during struggles—or, just as often, showing up for pain but avoiding joy. Both distort the connection.

Relational Betrayal: Failing to be loyal, honest, or consistent as a parent, partner, sibling, or friend. It quietly teaches, *You can't depend on me.*

Marital Betrayal: Infidelity, secrecy, and deception. Choosing gratification over commitment. It doesn't just break vows—it fractures the sense of safety love is meant to protect.

Betrayals of Identity

These betrayals don't just hurt your feelings—they dismantle your sense of self and belonging.

Identity Betrayal: Treating your core values, convictions, or individuality as inconvenient. It punishes integrity and rewards compliance.

Boundary Betrayal: Dismissing another person's right to privacy or autonomy with phrases like, "I'm the parent," or "That's just how I am." It teaches others that their limits don't matter, especially when authority is involved.

Narrative Betrayal: Rewriting the story to protect the image instead of the truth, and keeping the family reputation clean by erasing or distorting someone's reality. It silences the person who lived the pain and rewards those who deny it.

Betrayals of Responsibility

These occur when those entrusted to guide or protect instead cause harm, directly or indirectly.

Protective Betrayal: Failing to shield someone from danger. Excusing the abuser, minimizing the harm, or normalizing the toxic. It delivers one devastating message: "Your safety is not worth protecting at the expense of my discomfort."

Spiritual Betrayal: Using faith, morality, or authority to guilt, silence, or control. It replaces guidance with domination, wounding both the person's spirit and their trust in goodness itself.

Each of these forms leaves a mark, and they all share the same undercurrent: "You can't be safe in truth here." Healing begins when you stop silencing what's "right" in you to stay connected to what's "wrong" around you.

But here's the catch: betrayal doesn't always announce itself through actions. Sometimes, it whispers through tone, timing, or the stories people tell about you when you're not in the room. Sometimes, it hides behind laughter, or seeps through the pauses in a conversation where care should've been. That's when betrayal becomes language—when words stop protecting and start piercing.

* * *

🗣 When Words Wound

Betrayal doesn't always come through actions. Sometimes it's spoken *into* you.

Here are some examples of how words become weapons:

1. **Dismissive Language** – "You always overreact." → Encourages doubt in your feelings, leading you to stop sharing them.
2. **Gaslighting** – "That never happened." → Causes you to doubt your reality and gradually damages your sanity.
3. **Backhanded Praise & Sarcasm** – "Nice work . . . for someone like you." → Blurs genuine praise and harmful intent until you can't trust either. Leaves you uncertain about your standing with that person.
4. **Public Shaming** – Teasing or humiliating you in front of others. → Steals dignity while the crowd watches. This can impact how others perceive and interact with you.
5. **Undermining & Withholding** – Ignoring requests or punishing with silence. → Says, "You're not even worth a response," which can severely damage your dignity.
6. **Manipulation & Emotional Blackmail** – "After all I've done for you . . ." → Turns love into a tool for leverage. Manipulates you into feeling "thankful" for being mistreated and receiving less than what is fair.

A Familiar Pattern for Men

It's not just women who learn to shrink or over-function. I've also seen this pattern play out with men. They're told they're not leading enough, not doing enough, not carrying enough weight in the relationship. Yet when they try, their efforts are micromanaged, critiqued, or dismissed. One client shared how his wife asked him to clean the bathroom. He did it—but instead of appreciation, she demeaned him in front of their children for not doing it "the right way." It wasn't about the bathroom. It was about respect. He wanted a partnership, but what he experienced was control. Over time, he learned to step back—not because he didn't want to help, but because doing more only invited more criticism.

These aren't slips of the tongue; they're betrayals of dignity. Gradually, they teach you that your voice doesn't matter. And when you finally stop speaking, it's not because you ran out of words—it's because you ran out of faith that they'd be heard. But silence isn't the same as peace. It's a symptom of survival—a way to keep the room calm while your spirit stays crowded.

Over time, that silence becomes its own kind of betrayal: not of them, but of yourself. The real work of healing begins when you stop confusing composure with safety, and start rebuilding relationships—beginning with yourself—where respect doesn't have to be earned to be honored. When betrayal becomes habitual—spoken, subtle, and systemic—it doesn't just wound one person. It reconfigures the entire emotional ecosystem around them. What begins as silence between two people often expands into silence within families. And when that silence hardens into self-protection, love loses its structure. The result isn't just broken trust—it's a breakdown of safety, belonging, and identity that spans generations.

* * *

Betrayal and the Breakdown of Families

When betrayal becomes a pattern, it doesn't just fracture the connection—it corrodes the foundation that the connection was built on. It starts small: a secret here, a justification there, a comfort you tell yourself is harmless. But betrayal always grows. When it moves from words to actions, the impact multiplies.

Relational Fallout

A spouse who cheats does more than break a vow—they compromise their own integrity. They dishonor their partner, their children, and themselves. And the one they cheat with? They weren't chosen out of love, but out of access. Convenience isn't connection. Accessibility isn't affection. Genuine love never asks you to dishonor someone else to prove it exists.

Children: The Innocent Collateral Damage

When betrayal enters a family, children absorb the tremors first. They may not have the language for it, but they feel the fracture. A slammed door. A hollow dinner table. School grades that drop. A silence that hums louder than words. Infidelity isn't just an adult failure—it's a legacy that rewrites how children understand love, trust, and safety. The statistics only confirm what hearts already know:

- 75 percent of children feel lasting betrayal toward the parent who cheats.
- 80 percent say it changes how they view relationships.
- 70 percent struggle to trust others later in life.

But behind those numbers are the stories of sons and daughters learning how to love with caution—measuring safety before sincerity. They don't just inherit your last name, facial features, or quirks;

they inherit your blueprint for connection. And when that blueprint is drawn from betrayal, the pattern splits: some children become *prey*—over-accommodating, shrinking, performing to stay safe. Others become *predators*—controlling, dismissive, or emotionally detached, mistaking dominance for strength.

Both are reactions to the same wound. One avoids power to escape harm; the other abuses power to avoid feeling helpless. Either way, the message remains the same: love becomes a matter of survival, not safety.

💬 **Reflection Prompt:** Take a quiet moment to really look at your children—or even the younger version of yourself.

- Who are you raising, and what are you reinforcing?
- Are you teaching emotional awareness, or emotional servitude and manipulation?
- Are you cultivating a well-adjusted and balanced child—or creating another predator or prey?

Because *honor* is learned by observation, not instruction, it's passed down in how we use our power, tell the truth, and safeguard what's vulnerable and sacred—beginning within the family dynamic that teaches us what love and respect look like.

From Disrespect to Developmental Damage

The impact of betrayal doesn't end in the moment—it imprints patterns that echo across generations. Some inherit the habit of silence; others inherit the habit of control. Both grow from the same soil: dishonor.

Consequences of Family Betrayal

Betrayal Act	Disrespect to Self & Marriage	Child's Likely Response
Committing adultery	Breaks vows; dishonors truth	Distorts love and loyalty
Seeking outside attention	Devalues self and partner	Breaks trust; erodes sense of safety
Choosing image over truth	Chips away at self-confidence	Breeds future distrust

Self-Betrayal: The Silent Outcome of Tolerating

When betrayal becomes familiar, it doesn't just fracture relationships—it reshapes your relationship with yourself. Over time, you stop expecting protection. You stop asking to be noticed. You begin to shut down—on others and on yourself.

How They Relate to Self-Betrayal

- Ignore dignity → You question whether you deserve to exist with value.
- Doubt self-worth → You run on empty, relying on others for validation.
- Abandon respect → You stop communicating, and conflicts of disrespect increase.
- Dismiss self-respect → You hand over control and end up off course.
- Overreliance on self-esteem → You tie your worth to performance, chasing validation.
- Overextend your capacity → You push past limits, calling self-neglect "strength."

Together, these breakdowns lead to self-betrayal—treating yourself as an option rather than a priority. It rarely begins with a loud "no" to yourself. Instead, it starts with small compromises that *seem noble at the time*:

- Laughing off disrespect.
- Making yourself emotionally available to those who never reciprocate.
- Taking pride in being needed more than being nurtured.

You feel the warning signs but ignore them because confronting the issues feels too costly. You tell yourself, "It's not that bad," while you're quietly dying inside. You play roles instead of showing up as your whole self—because that's what's expected. When clarity breaks that cycle, it not only helps you see others for who they are, but it also allows you to see yourself for what you've been tolerating. And once you see it, you can't unsee it.

Returning to Integrity

With courage, you begin to shift—from guilt-driven yeses to boundaries that honor truth, from trying to be everything to everyone to being someone true to yourself, from over-explaining to simply saying, "This is enough." Clarity brings you back to yourself. It asks, gently but firmly: **Will you keep trading your dignity for temporary relief—or let integrity take the lead instead?**

Allowing integrity to lead means prioritizing alignment over avoidance—telling the truth even when silence seems easier, respecting your boundaries even when others call it selfish, and staying loyal to your values even when validation tempts you to compromise. As painful as betrayal feels, the most devastating kind isn't always what others did to you—it's what you start doing to yourself.

* * *

Culture-Induced Self-Betrayal

The moment you start betraying yourself, the world will hand you a script to make it look noble. It won't call it self-betrayal—it'll call it "empowerment." Today's culture promotes hyper-independence as strength:

- The self-made, closed-off millionaire who built an empire out of isolation to feel a sense of belonging.
- The #bossenergy that hides insecurity through ambition to feel superior.
- The curated feed of hustle till-you-drop by performing your worth one post at a time.

We built an altar to ambition and called it achievement. **"The dream is free, but the hustle is sold separately"** isn't inspiration—it's indoctrination. It teaches us that exhaustion is a sign of worth, that sacrifice is a currency for belonging, and that our humanity is negotiable as long as the dream is accomplished. This is the gospel of grind culture: salvation through self-betrayal, one to-do list at a time. **And because it preaches reward without rest, we trade our peace for applause and call it purpose.**

It appears shiny. It seems enviable. It even looks safe. But beneath the surface, the cost is high. Hyper-independence sacrifices intimacy for image, connection for control, and interdependence for performance. Many of us buy into it because independence feels safer than vulnerability, and hustle seems easier than honesty. **What the world calls "strength" often leaves us performing peace, negotiating self-worth, and mistaking exhaustion for excellence.**

When you buy into that script, the applause is instant—but the erosion is subtle. One day, you wake up armored but admired and wholly disconnected from yourself. You might recognize it in moments like these:

- **Dishonoring** your body because you're afraid that saying no makes you look uncommitted or replaceable.
- **Staying** too long in one-sided dynamics—personal or professional—because you're still hoping someone else will validate your worth.
- **Chasing** emotionally or strategically unavailable opportunities because being in motion feels safer than being still.
- **Silencing** your intuition in meetings, decisions, or relationships because compliance feels like the only way to keep the peace.
- **Overperforming** in roles that no longer fit because achievement still feels easier than authenticity.
- **Suppressing** your needs because, from the outside, quiet can appear to be alignment.
- **Lowering** the bar altogether because remaining numb feels less painful than facing their absence—or your own unmet potential.

That's the trade: **fake empowerment at the cost of clarity, dignity, and joy.** Beneath the shiny, enviable façade lies a debt that manifests in every performance. When culture teaches you that visibility equals value, you start curating yourself to survive. **You call it ambition or independence, but underneath, it's armor built from fear.** The applause becomes oxygen, and the mask becomes your livelihood. But the truth is that performance was never meant to replace design. What we build from fear will always collapse under the weight of authenticity.

* * *

The Illusion of Liberation

Female liberation has freed us right into submission. We traded corsets for contour palettes and cosmetic surgery—homemaking for hustle culture—dependence for debt. The old patriarchy said, "Be quiet." The new one says, "Be empowered"—but only if it's profitable, palatable, and postable. Real liberation isn't just the ability to choose—it's the ability to *opt out* without penalty. But we were never taught how to do that. We were taught how to do more, prove more, and *be* more. So we escaped their rules . . . and walked right into a different kind of obedience.

We won the battle but lost the war. We got the corner office, the paycheck, the platform—but somewhere along the climb, we traded liberation for labor. Freedom became another performance. We broke the glass ceiling, only to get cut on the shards. Maybe that glass wasn't all oppression—maybe it was protection. Perhaps all it needed was a little Windex. We escaped the kitchen, only to be imprisoned by calendars, deadlines, and curated perfection. We call it empowerment, but most days it feels like exhaustion in heels, oxfords, combat boots, and sneakers—because no matter the shoe, we're still running on fumes.

We were told independence would make us whole—but no one mentioned it might make us lonely. We've mistaken constant motion for progress, and applause for peace—equality for freedom. We're moving, but not forward. We're loud, but not heard. We're celebrated, but still unseen. Instead of motion, we're stuck. Instead of peace, we're in chaos. And at the forefront, we've allowed the applause of progress to chain us to performance. This—this right here—is one of the greatest scams, flimflams, and bamboozlements the world has willingly fallen for.

We didn't want to rule the world—we didn't want to be ruled. And this paradoxical irony; the very desire *not* to be ruled became the leash that bound us to a different kind of master: the illusion of liberation—same enslavement—two different masters. And as a wise proverb says: "You can't be a slave to two masters, for either he will hate the one and love the other, or he will stick to the one and despise the other." I see this struggle every week in my sessions—the grief on women's faces when realization hits: "Is this it? Is this what I fought so hard to get?" That moment alone debunks the myth that says, "You can have it all."

Perhaps those who say it mean sequentially—one season at a time, not simultaneously and instantly. But that's not how the world sells it to us. Each generation was told to do better than the one before, to climb higher, reach further, never rest, never stop. But when the mountain you're climbing has no peak, it becomes an exercise in futility. 'And that's precisely what you are doing if you believe you can show up 100% to everything. The myth that you can regularly be with your family, have fresh cookies baking, and simultaneously work sixty hours without expecting any balls to drop is unrealistic. We are all given the same twenty-four hours in a day.

You might ask, "So, Shante, what's the answer?" The survey says: **L.E.A.D.**

- Let humility increase your wisdom.
- Embrace love as your foundation of integrity.
- Accept your limitations.
- Develop contentment to guide your goals.

Because leadership without humility becomes domination, and domination can never have love as its foundation. Authentic leadership—of ourselves and others—begins when we stop trying to *have it all* and start learning to honor what's *enough*.

When Performance Takes Over Design

When performance replaces peace, design starts to malfunction. We don't just perform for the world—we perform in our relationships. The same impulse that drives us to prove our worth has taught us to compete where we were designed to connect. "You complete me." One of the most loved and mocked lines in film. Some swoon at its romance; others cringe, thinking it means you're not whole on your own. But what if it's one of the most honest, design-honoring truths ever spoken?

We're not made the same. Men often carry strength; women, endurance. Women remember with emotion; men reason with structure. These aren't flaws to fix—they're blueprints to respect. Not meant to divide us, but to connect us. This isn't about pigeon-holing anyone. A woman can be logical. A man can be deeply empathetic. But design works best when we *complement* rather than compete. Healthy teams thrive when each part contributes what the others lack. Yet it's in our closest, most intimate relationships that we resist this truth.

We fight where we were meant to fit. We compete where we were designed to complete. The point of *"you complete me"* isn't dependence—it's partnership. It's the humility to admit we weren't made to do life alone and the wisdom to see that strength multiplies when it's shared. Instead of respecting design, culture blurred the lines—then punished us for the confusion. Women are told to be nurturing yet productive, sexual yet modest, strong yet never too strong. Men are conditioned to lead without emotion, succeed without help, and prove manhood through performance. The result? A generation of women stretched thin, and a generation of men starved for honesty and connection. Both trapped in roles that deny their humanity—where repression is called strength and burnout passes for success.

This so-called "freedom" has resulted in emotional detachment. These roles devour identity. And beneath it all is grief—the sorrow of betraying our true design to survive in a world that doesn't nourish it. Over time, the genuine self fades, replaced by personas we mistake for strength.

When Femininity Turns Into a Performance

Womanhood has seen a significant shift in the past century—it's less about being and more about performing. We aren't just expected to feel deeply, but to appear flawless while doing it. To smile through discomfort. To stay desirable even when depleted. To be everything to everyone while hiding the parts of us that didn't fit the script. What looked like freedom was often just well-dressed survival. We mastered the art of composure, mistaking poise for power. Sass has become a shield. Sex is still a form of currency, but the shame that was once associated with it has been released. And what television shows and movies try to pass on as empowerment often conceals the quiet ache of wanting to be chosen, cherished, or seen. These weren't just women we grew up on; they were scripted roles, characters crafted to be admired, not understood. They showed us who to become, but never how to belong. Below, we'll look at some popular characters many of us were conditioned to imitate.

* * *

The Archetypes We Mirrored and the Ache Beneath Them

Why these women? Because they represent a particular mask of strength—what I call *liberation as performance*. Blanche, Maxine, Samantha, Lynn, and Issa were bold, witty, and unapologetically independent. They wore confidence like couture—stylish, sharp, unforgettable. They entertained us, but they also reinforced a dangerous cultural lie: that detachment is power, and independence is immunity from pain. By naming these women, I'm not celebrating their masks—I'm revealing the price we've paid for them.

Blanche Devereaux (The Golden Girls) – *The Flirtatious Performer*

Flirty, fabulous, and full of confidence, Blanche wore sexuality like armor. Beneath her bravado was the ache to be adored without having to constantly earn it. Her flirtation wasn't freedom—it was a distraction from loneliness and the fear of fading relevance.

Maxine Shaw (Living Single) – *The Guarded Achiever*

Brilliant, witty, and unflappable, Maxine embodied independence with style. Yet behind her intellect was a longing for connection she rarely admitted. Her strength was born of necessity, not choice—a shield against disappointment disguised as self-sufficiency.

Samantha Jones (Sex and the City) – *The Untouchable Liberator*

She crowned herself in sexual freedom—bold, in control, untamed. But behind the conquests was an aversion to vulnerability. Her "liberation" was self-protection, equating intimacy with danger. Independence was her fortress, even as it became her prison.

Lynn Searcy (Girlfriends) – *The Drifting Free Spirit*

Creative, bohemian, and boundless, Lynn seemed unrestrained. But her rootlessness wasn't freedom—it was flight. Beneath her easy charm was a deep craving for belonging she never stopped searching for.

Issa Dee (Insecure) – *The Conflicted Dreamer*

Funny, flirty, and "chill," Issa embodied contradiction—yearning for purpose while fearing exposure. She oscillated between clarity and confusion, her charm a mask for the self-doubt that haunted every choice she made.

These personalities wore liberation like a badge—unapologetically bold, sexually free, emotionally untethered. But behind the "I don't need anyone" mask was loneliness and longing—the ache of unresolved hurt dressed as autonomy. They weren't genuine role models. They were reflections of survival—roles written for applause, not for healing. And somewhere along the way, we forgot the difference.

But while women learned to perfect their performance, men learned to suppress theirs. Different stages—same script of survival.

* * *

When Masculinity Becomes a Mask

There's an unspoken grief men carry, too. It's just hidden behind different armor: stoicism, hyper-performance, emotional detachment, or performative dominance. Masculinity, at its healthiest, isn't the absence of emotion—it's the ability to express it with strength and integrity. But too often, it's misrepresented as a costume: toughness over tenderness, control over connection, womanizing over intimacy, and muting over self-expression.

From a young age, many boys are taught that their worth depends on what they *achieve,* rather than how they *feel.* They're praised for enduring pain, not for naming it. For taking care of everyone—except themselves. For conquering women instead of connecting with them. Over time, that pressure hardens into armor. And the armor becomes a mask. The result? Men who seem successful, composed, even "in control," but are quietly battling anxiety, depression, loneliness, and a grief they can't name. Not because they're unwilling to feel—but because they were never taught how to and weren't allowed to.

Why Father Figures?

By focusing on fathers, we see how these scripts of masculinity weren't merely personal—they became relational blueprints, passed down as legacies of survival, stoicism, perfection, or absence. And for those who grew up without a present or safe father, these on-screen men became silent teachers.

They filled the gaps left by real-life absence, modeling what love, leadership, and manhood were *supposed* to look like—even when those portrayals were incomplete or unhealthy. Even the more "balanced" fathers—those who tried to blend authority with affection—often modeled emotional control more than emotional presence. Through their performances, an entire generation learned to equate power with care, composure with strength, and dominance with respect—building identities around examples that were never meant to hold the full weight of truth.

James Evans (Good Times) – *The Survivalist Provider*

→ Survival through sacrifice. Born into poverty and systemic struggle, his strength was essential—but it came at the expense of tenderness. His silence was protection, but it left no room for vulnerability.

Heathcliff Huxtable (The Cosby Show) – *The Perfectionist*

→ Perfection through image. Marketed as the "ideal father," his humor and composure upheld respectability while masking deeper fragility. He modeled excellence, but the performance left little space for imperfection or emotional truth.

Danny Tanner (Full House) – *The Over-Compensator*

→ Control through grief. A grieving widower turned perfectionist, he channeled his loss into control. His love was genuine, but his need to "keep it clean" made emotional mess feel unsafe—order became his way of managing pain.

Tony Micelli (Who's the Boss) – *The Role Reverser*

→ Nurturing through service. A former athlete turned domestic caretaker, Tony embodied masculinity through service. He challenged gender norms, but his worth remained tied to usefulness—proof that even nurturance was measured in performance.

Tony Soprano (The Sopranos) – *The Power Prisoner*

→ Power through dominance. Violent, volatile, and seemingly in control, Tony mistook dominance for strength. His affairs weren't pleasure—they were power plays, attempts to fill the void that intimacy could not reach. Each conquest deepened his emptiness, confusing control with connection.

Frank Gallagher (Shameless) – *The Neglector*

→ Absence through neglect. Financially and emotionally absent, he abandoned his post as protector. His withdrawal forced the women and children to bear the burden, revealing what happens when self-interest replaces stewardship.

These TV personalities displayed strength while concealing their softness. They pursued control yet avoided vulnerability. They were vessels—reflections of what happens when men are taught that suppression is strength and stoicism is survival. What we call strength is often just a form of self-preservation. What we call stoicism is frequently hidden sorrow.

At some point, the roles became replacements for identity. Emotional suppression stopped being a coping mechanism and hardened into personality. Across families, relationships, and workplaces, people learned to hide in plain sight—not because they lacked depth, but because they were never taught how to reveal it safely. And that's where humility enters—not to make you smaller, but to reveal the version of you that doesn't need performance to prove worth. Because when clarity and respect fade, it's not just connection we lose—it's ourselves.

* * *

What Is Humility, and Why Is It So Misunderstood?

Now that we've clarified what self-respect and self-betrayal can look like, let's discuss another often misunderstood concept: humility. Many high-achieving, deeply spiritual, and emotionally intelligent people frequently confuse humility with invisibility. They downplay their talents, stay silent in rooms where they're qualified to speak, and believe that self-denial is a virtue. But humility was never intended to mean self-erasure.

In a world that values visibility, dominance, and self-promotion, humility is often mistaken for a sign of weakness. But true humility isn't about shrinking to make others comfortable. It's about understanding who you are—your strengths, flaws, gifts, and gaps—and choosing not to use that knowledge to manipulate, seek applause, or perform. Our culture is driven by constant productivity and "look-at-me" branding; as such, humility can seem outdated. Yet it's the posture that keeps us sane, genuine, and connected.

Still, humility isn't easy. Many fear it means being overlooked or taken advantage of. But humility is not humiliation. It isn't low self-worth or silence. It is integrity in action—living without competition or comparison. True humility involves discernment: knowing when to speak, when to yield, when to lead, and when to release. It fosters peace, not achievement. Since the world is strongly driven by ego, humility is often a radical act.

Client Vignette: The Conflict Between Humility and Visibility

I once coached a high-performing woman—a manager admired for her patience and diplomacy. In every meeting, she kept the peace, smoothed over conflict, and took on extra work without complaint. Her colleagues praised her for being "easy to work with," but what they didn't see was how often she silenced herself.

She was sharp and strategic, the kind of leader who saw around corners. Yet despite consistently offering clear solutions, her insights were often overlooked—until weeks later, when someone else repeated them and received the credit. Occasionally, her manager would resubmit her ideas in those same rooms without giving her the credit she deserved. After the meeting, she would thank him for bringing up her idea again. That's when he would privately acknowledge that he had "reshared" her contributions. But he never publicly announced they were hers. All too often, her ideas resurfaced without her name attached.

"I don't need the spotlight," she told me, "I just want my voice to matter." She wasn't seeking glory; she wanted to be heard. Her dilemma revealed the tension so many high-achieving women face: balancing humility with visibility—wanting their impact to speak for itself, yet longing for recognition that affirms their value and their worth. She wrestled with the question that sits at the intersection of grace and grit: **At what point does humility stop being noble and start becoming erasure?**

That question became the doorway to a more profound truth—one that reframes humility not as self-denial but as self-discipline. Not silence, but stewardship.

Purposeful Humility

Purposeful humility is the ability to understand your worth and still act with grace. It means recognizing your power without exploiting it, your voice without performing it. True humility doesn't shrink—it steadies. It doesn't hide—it honors. It is integrity expressed through self-discipline, not fear.

Real humility:

- Provides, but also safeguards.
- Leads when needed.
- Advocates for truth—both for others and for yourself.

Sometimes, being purposefully humble means knowing when to share your gifts—not to seek glory, but to serve. Humility isn't the absence of confidence. It's the wisdom to use your influence without losing your essence.

Humility Versus Hiding

In some families, humility was never modeled as a virtue—it was used as a muzzle. You were told to stay small, not to outshine, not to talk back. Confidence was called arrogance. Asking for what you needed was labeled as selfishness. So, you learned to hide your gifts, mute your light, and hope that someone else would validate them. But true humility doesn't deny your gifts—it honors their purpose. The real question isn't *whether* you should show up, but *why*. Is it meant to serve others? To open a door? To pass the torch? Or is it to seek praise, silence insecurity, or prove yourself?

Those questions keep your ego in check—but they should never silence your voice. Because when humility turns into hiding, the consequences don't stop with you; they ripple through generations.

Reframe: Clarity as a Legacy

Respect and betrayal aren't just personal—they become generational if left unchecked. Clarity breaks the cycle. When one person finally decides to face the truth—to name what was wrong and stop repeating it—they introduce clarity as a corrective force.

Clarity does three things:

- **Replaces silence with honesty.** The old rule was, "Don't talk about it." "Clarity says, "We can't heal what we won't name." It invites truth-telling into family and relational spaces where secrecy once ruled.

- **Replaces secrecy with safety.** Secrets create fear and shame. Safety grows when people are allowed to speak without punishment. Clarity fosters safety by enabling honesty without the fear of retribution.
- **Redefines legacy.** Instead of passing down dysfunction, you pass down awareness.

The lineage shifts—from survival and silence to honesty and healing.

And that's the real inheritance of healing. Not perfect families or flawless love, but a lineage that tells the truth and chooses to grow from it. Breaking the pattern isn't about fixing everyone who came before you—it's about becoming the first to stand in truth without shame. Because when one person chooses clarity over compliance, a new kind of strength enters the bloodline—principled love, deep respect, and genuine commitment. '

* * *

🌿 Emotional Arc – Chapter 4: Respect and Self-Betrayal

Core Tension

You've spent years being praised for your patience and ability to maintain peace. You learned to accept crumbs of consideration and call it loyalty—to see silence as humility and to measure your worth by how much you could give without expecting anything in return. Each time you crossed a boundary in the name of love, loyalty, or "being good," you betrayed yourself. And when betrayal became normalized—whether from others or within—you stopped expecting to be respected.

Positive Balance

Clarity reveals the truth: respect isn't just something you give—it's something you *live*. Boundaries aren't arrogance; they're architecture. They don't push love away—they protect it. Honor begins internally—in the words you use with yourself, the limits you uphold, and the truths you refuse to silence. When you live this way, you begin to attract people, environments, and opportunities that mirror that same integrity.

Empowering Tone

You don't have to keep proving your strength to deserve peace. You can walk in humility without erasing your identity. You can give freely without losing yourself. Let self-respect become the compass that guides your choices, conversations, and commitments. When you honor your dignity, you teach others how to do the same—and in doing so, you end the cycle of betrayal. Your clarity becomes your legacy.

* * *

Chapter 4 Summary and Closing: Respect and Self-Betrayal

Chapter 4 challenged you to do more than *understand* respect—it urged you to *embody* it. Not just in how you speak to others, but in how you talk to yourself. Not just in how you present yourself publicly, but in how you safeguard your peace privately. We examined the cost of confusing survival with love. We clarified the difference between self-worth, self-respect, and self-esteem—so you could stop abandoning yourself under the disguise of humility or harmony.

We also uncovered how betrayal often hides in plain sight. Sometimes it looks like peace when you're really suppressing pain. Other times it passes down through generations—disguised as performance, silence, or duty. We explored the roles you were taught to play—shaped by culture, trauma, and tradition—and asked the deeper question: *Who are you when you're not performing?*

This chapter invited you to reflect:

- What have I normalized to maintain unity?
- Where have I remained silent out of fear—not wisdom?
- What roles have I mastered at the expense of authenticity?
- Have I mistaken humility for hiding—or love for tolerating harm?

But it also gave you perspective. Clarity isn't just about seeing what's broken—it's about refusing to participate in your own undoing. Because respect isn't only a value—it's a practice. And integrity? That's the quiet strength that holds it all together. When you live aligned with that truth, your life becomes your voice—and it speaks with dignity even in silence.

✨ Chapter 4: Respect and Self-Betrayal – Pause for Perspective

Virtue: Honor

Honor begins with you. It's not just about how others treat you—but how you treat yourself in your quietest moments. Do your actions align with your values when no one's watching? Do your boundaries protect your dignity—or do you abandon them to avoid discomfort?

In relationships, honor means actively recognizing another person's worth—and protecting it without losing your own. Since we teach others how to treat us, honor sets the tone. It establishes expectations, prevents resentment, and creates space for mutual connection, not manipulation. Honor isn't naive loyalty or silent obedience—it's courageous alignment with truth.

In the workplace, integrity is evident in action. It's fulfilling commitments without sacrificing your values for validation or advancement. It's owning your missteps without deflecting blame. It's leading with respect—even when you disagree—and fostering environments where people feel safe to speak freely. Honor ensures your influence is rooted in dignity, not control. Because genuine respect doesn't demand attention—it commands it through consistency.

Honor teaches you to live with integrity; the next step is learning to live with *intimacy*—not just with others, but with yourself. Because once you've reclaimed respect, the next chapter of work begins: allowing yourself to be seen, felt, and known beyond the roles you've performed.

☞ Next Steps: Workbook Journal Prompts

For a deeper understanding of how respect—toward yourself and others—can break cycles of betrayal, refer to the companion workbook for Chapter 4.

 **Personal Notes & Insights**

Use this page to capture any quotes, ideas, or personal revelations that surfaced while reading. Let it be messy, real, and yours.

_____
_____
_____
_____
_____
_____
_____
_____
_____
_____
_____
_____
_____
_____
_____
_____
_____

SECTION TWO
FAKE SINCERITY

When you arrive, but it feels like a performance.

TO THE STRONG ONE WHO COULDN'T FALL APART

You were seen as strong, but rarely supported.

You are not Superwoman—contrary to what you've been conditioned to believe. This is for every time you said, "I'm not okay. I'm tired. I'm hurting," and someone replied, "You'll be fine. You're so strong." It's okay to admit that it stopped feeling like a compliment a long time ago. Now, when you hear it, you feel dismissed. Unseen. Unheard.

But with clarity, you finally realize: Resilience is sacred. It helps you endure your own burdens—and shows up for others with care, comfort, and wisdom. It creates space for compassion, not co-dependence. Being "so strong" was something altogether different. It meant taking on what was never yours to bear—their chaos, their comfort, their growth, their guilt.

Clarity teaches you this: Yes—we are called to help carry each other's burdens. But we are not meant to hold each other's loads. One fosters connection through sustainability. The other exhausts you and breeds resentment. You now understand the difference, and this understanding is your strength.

With clarity,
Shante

CHAPTER 5
EMOTIONAL AVAILABILITY AND THE FEAR OF BEING FELT

From guarded strength to open connection.

The previous chapter clarified how respect and betrayal shape our sense of worth and boundaries. However, self-respect has its limits if your emotions are still not under your control. You may recognize your worth, yet still keep your feelings hidden. You can stand up for yourself in principle, yet neglect yourself in practice. In many families, communities, and workplaces, "safety" was represented as composure, control, and predictability. The people around you may have rewarded your silence more than your honesty. And if you were "the strong one," your worth came from keeping it together—not from letting yourself be seen.

It appeared to be safe. It felt like a purpose. But it was actually suppressed. Here's the truth: clarity and worth are meaningless without emotional presence. If your emotions don't feel safe with you, they'll stay hidden behind old walls. And those walls aren't concerned with your growth—they're focused on your survival. This is where most people get stuck in their clarity journey:

- They acknowledge mistreatment but still downplay their feelings.
- They cease over-giving but never begin asking.

- They see the truth but still conceal it to maintain harmony.

So, what happens after you've reclaimed your worth—but still don't feel safe enough to express it? You live in half-truth. You hold the map but never take the road. You settle for "better than before." Emotional availability is the turning point. It's not just the capacity to care for others; it's the courage to let yourself be felt, by them and by you.

What Is Emotional Availability, Really?

Emotional availability goes beyond "being in touch with your feelings." It's the ability—and the willingness—to connect with your emotional truth, allow others to connect with it too, and make yourself emotionally accessible enough to understand theirs. It isn't about being endlessly open or sharing everything with everyone. It's about being present, honest, and engaged in ways that respect both your reality and your capacity—and make room for others to feel safe doing the same.

Two Aspects of Emotional Availability

1. Internal Availability

Your ability to:

- Acknowledge what you feel without rushing to fix or minimize it.
- Stay with discomfort long enough to learn from it.
- Feel before judging your emotions as "good" or "bad."

Internal availability is self-connection. It's the moment you stop abandoning yourself to make your feelings more acceptable—to others or to you.

2. Relational Availability

Your ability to:

- Share your feelings with trusted people without over-editing or apologizing.
- Be emotionally **accessible** enough to understand and respond to others' emotions with care and accuracy.
- Accept others' feelings without judgment, control, or avoidance.
- Embrace the discomfort of mutual vulnerability instead of retreating into performance or problem-solving.

Relational availability is emotional presence in motion. It's not about oversharing or flooding people with raw emotion—it's about showing up as your whole self while creating space for others to do the same. When both people practice relational availability, communication shifts from performance to participation. You stop waiting to be understood and start engaging in mutual understanding—the kind that deepens trust, not dependence.

This is your ability to:

- Share your feelings with trusted people, without over-editing or apologizing for them.
- Accept others' emotions without judgment, control, or avoidance.
- Embrace the discomfort of mutual vulnerability instead of withdrawing into performance or problem-solving.

Relational availability refers to the emotional presence one exhibits while engaging. It's not about oversharing or flooding people with raw emotion—it's about showing up as your whole self in ways that deepen mutual trust and intimacy. But emotional availability has limits. It requires discernment—knowing when your openness builds connection and when it becomes self-exposure that leaves you drained or misunderstood. Without that discernment, what begins as authenticity can quietly turn into performance.

What Emotional Availability Is Not

- Oversharing in hopes of rescue
- Emotional dumping without considering others' capacity
- Self-erasure disguised as "openness"
- Calm composure that conceals the truth
- Over-intellectualizing feelings until they lose meaning

When you're emotionally available, you don't perform your feelings just to be heard—or justify them to make them valid. You express what's real without watering it down for others' comfort. And you can accept others' truths without making them about you.

Why It Matters

Emotional availability isn't about saying what's "right"—it's about being real with what matters. The first step in being real is recognizing what you actually feel. When you can name it, you can confront it. When you confront it, you can feel it. And when you can feel it, you can transform it. Let's start by naming the emotions that most often shape—or cloud—our clarity.

* * *

Emotional Forces: How Feelings Distort or Develop Clarity

You can't be emotionally available if you lack the language to name and navigate your feelings. Every emotion has two sides: one that clouds vision, and one that clarifies it. What distorts clarity when left unexamined can also develop wisdom when acknowledged.

Jealousy ↔ Envy

When it distorts clarity:

It fixates on what others have, shifting your gaze outward instead of inward. Unchecked, jealousy morphs into envy—resenting others' success and losing sight of your own growth. At its most harmful, envy turns darker: "If I can't have it, you shouldn't either." This is when clarity is most at risk, because you start measuring your worth by someone else's wins.

When it develops clarity:

It reveals what you truly value. When explored rather than suppressed, jealousy can reveal hidden desires or unmet dreams that deserve your attention. It can also expose buried resentments you haven't named. Awareness transforms comparison into curiosity: *What is this emotion showing me about what I want to create—or what I need to address?*

Clarity requires a clear view of your path—and you can't run your race if your eyes stay fixed on someone else's lane.

Discouragement ↔ Hope

When it distorts clarity:

Discouragement convinces you that setbacks define your worth. It narrows your vision and whispers worst-case scenarios until they feel like reality. Left unchecked, it replaces curiosity with fear and makes rest feel like failure. It tempts you to stop before the lesson is complete—to abandon progress because you can't yet see the payoff.

When it develops clarity:

Discouragement is not a verdict—it's a signal. It often points to a lack of capacity, clarity, or community. When acknowledged early, it becomes a map: showing where to pause, re-evaluate, or ask for help. That's where **hope** becomes the corrective lens. Hope isn't naïve optimism or "good vibes only"—it's the grounded expectation of good combined with a willingness to keep moving toward it. It restores perspective by widening what discouragement has narrowed. Together, discouragement and hope shape your clarity: one warns you where you're depleted; the other reminds you where you're still becoming.

The goal isn't to silence discouragement—it's to let hope speak louder.

Longing ↔ Resentment

When it distorts clarity:

It keeps you tethered to the past or longing for what may never return. When unexamined, longing can morph into entitlement—convincing you that you're owed something that was never meant to be yours. Unmet longing can fester into resentment when you've over-given, under-received, or been ignored. Both emotions cloud perception: one idealizes what's missing; the other indicts what's present. Left unchecked, they make it hard to tell whether your pain comes from appropriate desire or misplaced expectation.

When it develops clarity:

Longing, when honored, reveals what matters most. It's a mirror reflecting your values, not a magnet for comparison. Resentment, when examined honestly, becomes a form of feedback—it reveals where your expectations and reality have diverged. Together, they expose the gap between desire and reality—between the places you've given too much and the places you've expected too much.

Longing asks, *What am I truly yearning for—or coveting?*

Resentment asks, *Where have I given beyond what was honored—and where have I expected what wasn't promised?*

Clarity grows when you stop living in the ache of "almost" and begin moving toward the peace of "enough."

Understanding emotion is one step; expressing it safely is another. When emotional expression feels risky, we tend to adapt by concealing our feelings rather than connecting with others. That's how emotional unavailability begins—not from lack of feeling, but from fear of consequence.

* * *

Unavailable by Design: The Protective Pattern

Now that you have language for emotions that shape or block your clarity, it's time to ask a more nuanced question: If these feelings are so important to recognize, why do so many of us hide them?

The answer isn't always weakness. Often, it's because of a pattern. You learned to read the room, predict reactions, and protect yourself from pain. These habits once kept you safe—but what protected you then might now prevent your peace. The same walls that once served as shelter may have quietly become a prison.

Why We Learn to Conceal Our Feelings

In some families, communities, and workplaces, emotional expression wasn't just frowned upon—it was risky. Speaking up invited ridicule. Showing hurt invited rejection. Vulnerability became unsafe.

So, you adapted:

- You smiled when you were angry.
- You made jokes when you wanted to cry.
- You held yourself together while falling apart inside.

Emotional suppression isn't indifference—it's survival. It's the body's way of saying, "Not here. Not yet."

The Five Fears That Lead to Emotional Unavailability

Fear of Abandonment – "If you see how I really feel, you'll leave. Because it's too much."

This fear convinces you that honesty will cost you love, so you withhold truth to preserve belonging.

Fear of Rejection – "If I share this, you won't see me the same anymore. And our bond might be damaged." You silence yourself to protect the version of you others approve of—even when that silence costs authenticity.

Fear of Judgment – "If I'm honest, you'll see me as weak, dramatic, or unstable. I'm expected to be the strong one." You perform strength to protect credibility, turning vulnerability into a private luxury you can't afford.

Fear of Being Misunderstood – "If I tell you what's real, you'll twist it, dismiss it, or take it the wrong way." It teaches you to withhold or overexplain to prevent misinterpretation, trading authenticity for constant validation.

Fear of Losing Control – "If I reveal too much, I'll lose my grip on how I'm seen—or how this goes." It teaches you to manage tone, narrative, and your reactions to keep your power and control over outcomes.

Each fear teaches the same lesson: **it's safer to hide than to be seen.**

The Motive Behind the Mask

When connection lacks authenticity, it turns into control—either controlling how the other person sees you or controlling the space so truth can't breathe. The latter is emotional choreography. It's managing tone, timing, and temperature so nothing feels unsafe or unpredictable. It sounds like laughter when a moment gets too heavy. It appears to be smoothing out tension before it can surface. It feels like peace, but it's really performance. You're not avoiding conflict—you're postponing clarity. You're not keeping peace—you're keeping truth at bay because love can't survive in a room where honesty can't be shared. Every mask begins with fear. But not every fear has the same origin—or the same outcome.

Both versions are trauma-born, yet they evolve in opposite directions. For some, the mask is a form of **self-preservation**. It's fear rooted in pain—the kind that learns to stay small to stay safe. It hides not to deceive, but to protect what's sacred. This mask guards vulnerability that is born from rejection, dismissal, or punishment for emotional truth. It's a quiet fear that says, "If I'm honest, I might be hurt."

For others, the mask is a form of **self-deception**. It's fear rooted in control—the kind that manipulates reality before it can be threatened. They deceive others because they've already deceived themselves. Charm becomes camouflage, empathy becomes bait. This mask doesn't guard vulnerability—it exploits it. It studies your openness, mirrors your needs, and markets a false sense of safety to maintain control.

Both wear composure well. Both crave safety. But one hides to preserve authenticity; the other hides to possess it—to rewrite what's real and rule the narrative. One is born from the fear of being hurt; the other, from the fear of being powerless. Both deserve understanding—but only one has the potential to lead to healthy and mutual availability.

When masking becomes a way of life, it doesn't just shape your emotions—it shapes your identity. And for many, that identity takes the form of strength.

* * *

The Role of Identity: The "Strong One"

If you were the dependable one, the problem-solver, the caretaker, you might have built your entire identity around being strong. People looked to you for support, not the other way around. This role offers validation, but it also confines you.

- You feel pressure to stay steady, even when you're hurting.
- You hide so you don't "burden" anyone.
- You show empathy, but you seldom receive it in return.

Being the "strong one" may feel empowering because you are viewed as being in control, but it's often an emotional exile—from others and from yourself. It usually appears as emotional distance disguised as stability. But identity doesn't disappear just because you outgrow its origin. The "strong one" role becomes so familiar that it feels natural—even necessary. That's how the pattern quietly sustains itself.

How the Pattern Maintains Its Existence

The problem with intentionally being unavailable is that it initially appears to work.

- You steer clear of conflict.
- You guard yourself against immediate pain.
- You keep an image that feels safe to you and acceptable to others.

But over time, the expenses increase:

- Your relationships seem superficial or unbalanced.
- You steer clear of conflict.
- You preserve an image that feels safe to you and acceptable to others.
- You lose sight of what you truly want and need.
- You incorrectly label withdrawal as restoration.

Client Vignette: The Class Clown Shield

One client I worked with described himself as the "class clown" during his childhood. Humor was his armor. Whenever tension rose at home, he would crack a joke. Laughter became the family's release valve—and his role was to provide it. As an adult, that role followed him. In meetings, with friends, even in relationships, he could make people laugh—but when it came to expressing disappointment, grief, or real need, he shut down.

Joking was safer than being honest. People saw him as lighthearted, easygoing, always fun to be around—but underneath, he often felt unseen and unsupported. This is how emotional unavailability can disguise itself. It doesn't always look like silence or withdrawal. Sometimes it's being "on" for everyone else—keeping things entertaining and light—while avoiding the conversations that truly matter.

Micro-Avoidance Behaviors: The Subtle Shields

Emotional unavailability doesn't always appear as pulling away. Sometimes it feels like being present—but only on controlled, "safe" terms (see Chapter 1).

- Making jokes when a moment becomes too vulnerable
- Keeping things "light" to avoid heavy topics
- Giving advice instead of showing empathy
- Masking chaos with charm, skill, or composure
- Changing the subject when the truth gets too close

Protecting prevents presence: Emotional availability depends on presence, and presence can't happen when you're stuck in protection mode.

Protection is about control: It's about scanning for danger, managing impressions, and guarding the most vulnerable parts of yourself so they can't be hurt.

Presence is about connection: It's about showing up as you are, without needing to edit, explain, or hide the truth of what you feel. When you're in protection mode, your attention is divided—you're thinking about what's safe to share, how it might be received, and if it will cost you too much. You may seem calm, engaged, even open, but part of you is watching from the sidelines, making sure no one gets too close. It's about bringing your whole self into the room—body, mind, and emotions—without façade or distance. It doesn't mean being reckless with your truth; it means being real with it.

Here's the paradox: protection prevents pain, but it also prevents depth. You can't be known and guarded at the same time. So while protection might keep you safe, it also keeps you isolated. When that happens, emotional expression quietly gives way to emotional presentation. The goal shifts from being *understood* to being *approved of*. And when protection becomes habitual, even your honesty starts to filter itself—you don't just hide what hurts; you reshape it to sound reasonable. That's where emotional justification begins.

* * *

Understanding Versus Justifying Your Emotions

Emotional availability starts with honesty—not only with others but also with yourself. That honesty can lead down two very different paths: understanding your emotions or justifying them.

Understanding equals self-awareness. It sounds like: What am I feeling? Where did it come from? What is it asking of me? It's rooted in curiosity, not fear. You let the emotion exist without rushing to fix, minimize, or prove it. You're not performing; you're listening.

Justifying equals self-defense. It feels like you have to argue your case before you're allowed to hurt. It sounds like: Here's why I'm upset . . . here's the evidence . . . please believe me. Justifying turns feelings into performances—softened for comfort, edited for favor, or exaggerated for credibility. If you have to explain your pain for it to count, you've been taught that your emotions need permission.

How to recognize justification creeping in:

- You focus more on backstory than feelings.
- You mentally pre-answer objections before speaking.
- You rush to explain things to others before you understand them yourself.
- You wait for reassurance or confirmation before trusting your own judgment.

Example (Family Dynamic)

You tell a sibling, "I felt really hurt when you canceled on me at the last minute." Instead of letting the truth land, you immediately add, "I know you've been busy with work, and I'm probably just overreacting, and it's not like I had anything that important planned . . ." By the time you finish, you've rewritten the moment to make it easier for them—softening your hurt so they won't feel guilty, preemptively shrinking so you won't be dismissed. The feeling you wanted to share has been buried under proof that it's "not a big deal."

Understanding and explaining your feelings for their clarity is one thing, but justifying your emotions always depends on others' permission. We'll explore the related pattern of over-explaining more deeply in Chapter 8. For now, remember: closeness doesn't require a closing argument.

The more you justify, the more you train yourself to believe that trust must be earned—only after you've proven you're safe to love. But trust doesn't start there. To be emotionally available, you have to identify which kind of trust you're dealing with—and what happens when the wrong one takes the lead.

* * *

Why Trust Is Important for Emotional Availability

You can't stay isolated and expect clarity in relationships—yet opening every door without discernment leaves you exposed. Balance begins with self-trust: it gives you the courage to open wisely, the wisdom to hold back when needed, and the strength to close doors that don't serve you.

The Trust Spectrum

- **Self-Trust – Your Foundation:** Confidence in your own judgment and ability to respond. It ensures that availability is safe, so you know when and to whom you can open up and when to trust someone's reliability without needing constant proof. It encourages vulnerability while remaining vigilant to potential red flags.
- **Trust – The Open Door:** Belief in someone's reliability without needing proof all the time. It invites vulnerability but remains cautious of red flags.
- **Blind Trust – The Unlocked Door at Night:** Trust given without proof of reliability. Often based on habit or hope, it leaves you open to harm or disappointment.
- **Entrust – Giving the Keys to Someone Else:** An intentional decision to place your care and resources in the hands of someone who has earned it—without losing your control.
- **Mistrust – The Hesitant Handshake:** Caution driven by past hurt. You open slowly, test consistency, and share cautiously.
- **Distrust – The Locked Gate:** Default to doubt. Assumes deception or harm, making bonding nearly impossible because protection takes precedence.

Trust opens the door, but safety determines whether you'll walk through it. Sometimes, the barrier isn't others' trustworthiness—it's your own readiness to feel safe being fully known. You can trust someone's intentions, yet still keep your guard up because the parts of you that once had to hide haven't learned what safety feels like yet.

Emotional availability isn't just about opening up; it's about learning where your openness can land safely. That's where many of us get stuck—mistaking a quick connection for safety, or attention for depth.

* * *

Transitioning from Availability to Safety

Many of us have learned how to open up, but not how to stay open safely. And that's where confusion begins.

If I asked most men and women I know, they'd admit they've been drawn to someone emotionally unavailable or unsafe at some point. We often mistake unpredictability for passion, or distance for a challenge—when in truth, we're replaying old patterns that feel familiar. Emotional unavailability wears many masks: charm without consistency, vulnerability without follow-through, connection without commitment. It's often how situationships begin—with intensity rather than intimacy.

The real confusion happens when attention feels like intimacy but isn't rooted in reality. What you're responding to isn't depth—it's presentation. And that's why safety matters. Safety is the foundation that makes availability sustainable. Without it, even good intentions collapse under fear.

Because no matter how much two people care, fear will always distort the connection. It turns openness into overthinking, honesty into hesitation, and love into strategy. When you don't feel safe, you start performing—filtering your truth to protect your heart. The relationship might still look healthy on the surface, but beneath the surface, every interaction becomes a negotiation between comfort and authenticity. Fear builds walls where trust was supposed to grow roots.

The difference between **intensity** and **intimacy** is this: safety is the space where you can take emotional risks without being mocked, minimized, or dismissed. When safety is present, availability stops being performance—and becomes a steady choice.

Quick Safety Check-In

Think of one meaningful relationship in your life and ask yourself:

- When I share my truth, do I feel heard—or handled?
- Do I edit my emotions to protect peace, or express them to build trust?
- Do I trust myself to name when something feels unsafe, even if no one else sees it?
- Do I know how to rebuild safety when it's been broken—or do I wait for others to fix it first?

If any of these answers feel uncertain, your safety may be compromised, and your availability may be performing under pressure. Because safety isn't built through isolated reassurance; it's revealed through consistent behavior. It's not only something you receive; it's something you help create.

True safety begins within, but it's strengthened through practice—how you show up, repair, and remain open even when it would be easier to retreat. It's what transforms emotional availability from a moment into a way of being. Later, in Chapter 8, we'll explore what safety looks like in practice—how to build it, recognize it, and sustain it. Safety makes emotional availability possible—but consistency, alignment, and integrity make it last. It's one thing to open up; it's another to stay open without losing yourself. That kind of endurance doesn't come from effort alone—it comes from strength.

The Ache of Being Forgotten

Even with all the insight in the world, awareness can't always protect you from the ache of invisibility. You can spend so long learning how to be safe that you forget how to be seen. What once felt like discernment slowly becomes distance. The only thing worse than not being seen is being overlooked. Not being seen hurts—but being erased from memory makes you question your worth, your presence, and your impact (whether personally or professionally).

You gave your best sincerely, yet somehow disappeared after you provided what was needed. Your contribution is quickly forgotten, even when it's a key piece of a person's or organization's success. It's a grief that convinces you maybe you never existed to them at all. And that's where rebuilding begins—not through more performance, but through rediscovery.

From Being Forgotten to Finding Yourself

That realization—of giving so much and still disappearing—forced me to ask, *Who am I when I'm not performing for belonging?* In 2016, the CliftonStrengths Assessment gave me something I didn't know I needed: language for what was right about me, not just what needed fixing. It helped me see that my desire for partnership wasn't weakness—it was design. That my hunger to learn wasn't arrogance—it was curiosity seeking connection. Understanding my strengths revealed that my brokenness was really a misdirection. I always had what I needed to succeed, but I had been using my best traits in survival mode. With awareness, I could finally use them in alignment.

* * *

From "Being Strong" to Living Your Strengths

Feeling safe enough to be available is only part of the equation. The other part is understanding how to show up once you're there. For many of us, being *the strong one* has been our identity—strong enough to carry everything, strong enough never to ask for help. It sounds noble, but "strong" often covers exhaustion, isolation, and quiet resentment. Strength should be viewed as a resource, not a disguise.

Endurance is one of the purest forms of strength. It's the steady power that allows you to withstand uncertainty, loss, or hardship without losing your center. At its best, endurance is fueled by hope and grounded in wisdom—it helps you persevere when the outcome is unclear. But endurance was never meant to be the whole story. When it becomes your only goal, it stops being a passage and turns into a posture. You start enduring everything, even what was never meant to be permanent. You stop reaching for growth because survival feels like a form of growth.

That's the trap of "being strong." You carry it all, fix it all, hold it all—until your strength becomes a cage. Endurance isn't meant to erase you; it refines you. It's the bridge between hardship and growth, but it was never meant to be the destination. If you're reading this book, you've probably already learned how to withstand the complexities of life. The next step is to engage with them.

Here's the shift: Living in strength.

Endurance steadies you through storms; strength equips you to build after they pass. Living in strength doesn't mean abandoning grit—it means expanding beyond it. It's what happens when resilience meets intention, when perseverance becomes partnership, and when you stop surviving *through* strength and start living *from* it. Living in strength still delivers excellence but adds balance. It means holding what's yours, sharing what's not, and drawing from your full range of strengths rather than relying on grit alone.

Gallup's *CliftonStrengths* identifies four domains that describe how we naturally feel, think, and behave—**Executing, Strategic Thinking, Relationship Building, and Influencing.** These principles don't just apply to leadership; they reflect how you navigate life, manage your energy, and maintain connections. Each domain reveals both your brilliance and your blind spots—how your strength sustains you when grounded in clarity, and how it strains you when driven by fear. Endurance is never the problem; instead, it's imbalance.

Strength turns into a struggle only when it operates without rest, reflection, or reciprocity.

Here's what that shift looks like when you move from *being strong* to *living in strength:*

- **Execution-Driven:** "Being strong" means taking responsibility for everything—making sure it's done right, even if it costs your peace. *Living in strength* means performing with excellence while allowing others to carry their share, trusting partnership without sacrificing standards.
- **Strategic Thinking:** "Being strong" means generating endless solutions and wanting to have them implemented. *Living in strength* means choosing what matters most—prioritizing insight over overload, delegation over depletion, and clarity over control.
- **Relationship-Focused:** "Being strong" means pouring endlessly into others while neglecting yourself. *Living in strength* means giving without erasing, surrounding yourself with people who both receive and replenish.
- **Influence-Driven:** "Being strong" means always staying "on"—the motivator, the light, the voice. *Living in strength* means knowing when to speak and when to step back, allowing your influence to rest in authenticity rather than performance.

Whether at work, in relationships, or within yourself, living in strength means leading with awareness. It's not about pushing harder; it's about applying wisdom to your effort. And that's where emotional intelligence comes in—because even your greatest strengths need sensitivity to context. EQ helps you know when to lean in, pause, and step away. It's the awareness that keeps your strength human and your presence balanced.

* * *

Why This Matters for Emotional Availability

Emotional intelligence (EQ) is the ability to recognize, understand, and manage emotions—both your own and others'—and to use that awareness to guide your behavior and relationships with wisdom. It bridges emotional honesty and emotional safety, helping you stay open without losing grounding.

IQ helps you process information; EQ enables you to process people—including yourself. It turns awareness into agility. Without it, emotional availability becomes reactive—either overly exposed or completely withdrawn. EQ matters because it:

- **Helps you read emotional context**—picking up on tone, tension, and energy so you know when to speak, pause, or listen.
- **Guides emotional regulation**—allowing you to express what's real without flooding others or numbing yourself.
- **Protects boundaries without building walls**—helping you stay present without losing peace.
- **Turns endurance into engagement**—transforming resilience into responsiveness instead of reactivity.

When EQ and endurance work together, they create balance: endurance steadies you, and EQ attunes you. Together, they make emotional availability a skill you can sustain—not just a feeling you hope to maintain. That's where a strengths-based approach becomes powerful. It moves you from simply functioning to fully engaging—using your strengths to deepen connection rather than disguise its absence.

Reflective Prompts

- What strengths do you rely on only when things go wrong?
- What strengths could help you succeed when things go well?

- Where are you relying on endurance instead of expanding into growth?

Your strengths are tools—but in survival mode, they turn into armor. Living in strength isn't just about *what* you do; it's about *how* you feel and respond while doing it. When endurance provides stability and EQ brings sensitivity, availability becomes something you embody—not something you fight to keep.

* * *

EQ: The Toolkit for Emotional Availability

Think of EQ as the difference between owning power tools and actually knowing how to use them without wrecking the house—or yourself. Emotional intelligence is the *instruction manual* for availability. It tells you when to open up, how to stay grounded, and how to connect without losing your center.

When applied, EQ transforms emotional honesty into emotional maturity.

It helps you manage intensity without dulling authenticity, and discern when openness invites growth versus when it invites harm.

The Five Core Tools:

1. **Self-Awareness**—Recognizing and accurately naming your emotions; understanding how they shape your choices, tone, and timing.
2. **Self-Regulation**—Managing impulses, staying calm under pressure, and acting from values instead of reactions.
3. **Empathy**—Reading and honoring others' emotions—spoken or unspoken—without absorbing them.

4. **Social Skill**—Building trust through communication, adaptability, and genuine collaboration.
5. **Motivation**—Staying grounded in purpose and growth, not performance or approval.

When these tools work together, they turn awareness into wisdom. You start noticing patterns—both yours and others'—and instead of reacting to emotion, you respond with clarity.

Quick Reflection:

1. *In your most stressful moments, did you act according to your values—or react to protect your ego?*
2. *Did the people around you leave that moment feeling seen or more cautious?*
3. *What would it look like to bring calm and clarity to tension without losing your honesty?*

Visualize two people under pressure:

One pushes through, focused only on endurance. They're strong, but hard to reach. The other stays aware of the room, listens for what's unspoken, and adjusts tone to invite truth. Both are capable—but only one is emotionally available. That's the difference EQ makes. It's the quiet precision that turns endurance into engagement, and strength into safety.

Emotional availability without EQ is like a car without a steering wheel—you can have power but no direction. EQ gives that power purpose. It helps you read the emotional terrain and navigate relationships more successfully. It's what allows clarity to do its real work—turning knowledge into connection, endurance into empathy, and strength into presence. Because in the end, availability isn't measured by how much you reveal, but by how deeply you can relate.

And that's what this section is meant to lead you toward:

Not just *feeling everything*, but *understanding what your feelings are here to teach you*.

Not just *enduring life*, but *engaging with it*—honestly, wisely, and with emotional integrity.

Reframe: Using Clarity as Permission

- Emotional availability is not a weakness; it's alignment.
- Establishing agreements does not hinder intimacy; it enables it.
- Strength doesn't have to mean silence; it can mean being seen.
- Safety isn't numbness; it's trust.
- Openness isn't surrender; it's a choice.

Every chapter in this book builds toward wholeness—but this one asks for courage. It's where your strength meets your softness, and your intellect finally yields to intimacy. The next layer of clarity isn't about what you know—it's about what you're willing to feel.

* * *

꩜ Emotional Arc – Chapter 5: Emotional Availability and the Fear of Being Felt

Core Tension

You've reclaimed your worth, but you're still holding your breath. You speak up in theory but go silent when it matters most. You've stopped over-giving, yet you still struggle to receive. The fear isn't about being unworthy anymore—it's about *feeling* that worth. After years of survival, being truly seen can feel more dangerous than being invisible.

Positive Balance

Emotional availability isn't about opening the doors wide to everyone—it's about knowing who gets the key and trusting yourself to change the locks when necessary. It's the courage to be seen without overexposing yourself, to connect without performing, and to offer presence that's both genuine and mutual. When you trust yourself to hold your emotions responsibly, openness stops being a risk and becomes an act of alignment.

Empowering Tone

This is where strength stops being a shield and becomes a bridge—where endurance partners with growth. Here, trust in yourself becomes the safety net that lets you show up fully without losing yourself. Emotional availability isn't a gift handed out freely; it's a conscious practice that turns clarity into connection, resilience into intimacy, and survival into participation.

* * *

Chapter 5 Summary and Closing: Emotional Availability and the Fear of Being Felt

Chapter 5 invited you to move beyond being *strong*—to become *available*. Not just during calm moments, but especially in the uncomfortable ones where withdrawal feels safer than honesty. Not only for others, but also for yourself—because presence without preservation isn't sustainable.

We explored the shift from performing strength to living from your strengths—where endurance harmonizes with growth, rather than competing with it. We uncovered the cost of survival-based living: guardedness, exhaustion, and surface-level connection. We examined how trust—particularly self-trust—creates the foundation for safety and openness. And we asked the more complex questions that shape emotional maturity:

- Where am I relying on endurance instead of growth?
- How often does my strength prevent me from being seen?
- Do I know the difference between feeling safe and feeling numb?
- What would change if I used my strengths to connect rather than to cope?

We redefined availability as a *choice*—not a risk. Emotional availability enables you to engage deeply without feeling depleted. It transforms clarity into connection and turns trust into a sustainable practice. You no longer have to brace against life; you can participate in it. Being felt isn't your weakness—it's your freedom.

✦ Chapter 5: Emotional Availability and the Fear of Being Felt – Pause for Perspective

Virtue: Hospitality of Heart

Being kind to yourself begins with creating an inner space where your emotions are welcomed, not rushed, silenced, or shamed. It's the practice of sitting with what you feel—joy, sadness, doubt, or longing—without judgment. Emotional openness starts here: choosing curiosity over criticism and inviting yourself to take a seat at your own table.

Hospitality in relationships is the art of creating room for others to be fully seen and felt—without the pressure to fix, manage, or control them. It's presence without pretense, listening without an agenda, and respecting the natural pace of trust. Genuine hospitality also requires allowing yourself to be seen, even when vulnerability feels inconvenient. Mutual trust can only grow where both hearts are visible.

In the workplace, hospitality translates into psychological safety. It means fostering environments where people feel accepted as they are—where ideas can be voiced without fear, and feedback can be shared with respect. For leaders, it's the balance of empathy and clarity: encouraging diverse perspectives, honoring contributions, and upholding commitments that make the space safe for truth. Genuine professional hospitality isn't about comfort—it's about cultivating belonging that strengthens both people and performance.

Hospitality of heart is the beginning of wisdom—where openness learns to coexist with discernment. To welcome life as it comes is grace; to honor what it takes from you is truth. To live with an open heart is to learn this rhythm—how to stay tender without surrendering your boundaries.

☞ Next Steps: Workbook Journal Prompts

For a deeper understanding of how emotional availability begins within yourself and affects every connection you make, refer to the companion workbook for Chapter 5.

 **Personal Notes & Insights**

Use this page to capture any quotes, ideas, or personal revelations that surfaced while reading. Let it be messy, real, and yours.

TO THE ONE WHO MEANT WELL BUT COULDN'T SEE ME

Gratitude should set you free, not bind you.

You were there. Present in body. Reliable in your role. Faithful in doing what needed to be done. But when you looked into my eyes, you could only see *yourself*. Through the unspoken rules of survival, I had to earn your love. And in doing so, I never had the chance to develop my voice. I became what was secure, helpful, easy, and safe. That conditioning, I now recognize, has shaped my identity in many ways.

Love was clouded by obligation, and I was left feeling guilty for simply existing. I learned to shrink, to quiet my ache, to mold myself into someone who doesn't take up too much space. You might have meant well, and you may even believe you were loving me. Perhaps you were in the only way you knew how.

But with clarity, I'm learning how to appreciate what you could give while acknowledging the hurt that came with it. I'm embracing gratitude that liberates me, rather than gratitude that confines me. I no longer confuse being used with being recognized. And I've begun reclaiming and redefining the parts of me that were buried underneath all the roles I was praised for playing.

With clarity,
Shante

CHAPTER 6
GRATITUDE AND RESENTMENT

You can recognize the good without justifying the harm.

Chapter 5 explored *emotional availability and the fear of being felt.* It wasn't just about letting others in—it was about finally allowing yourself to register the truth of what you feel. The grief, the anger, the tenderness, the longing you've muted to survive. It revealed that safety begins when you stop managing your emotions and start meeting them with honesty. But once you allow yourself to be felt—by you and by others—something subtle happens. People begin to project what they want to feel *through* you. They expect warmth without confrontation, empathy without boundaries, forgiveness without repair. **Gratitude becomes the proof that you're "healed," letting them off the hook.**

That's where **Chapter 6** begins. Because openness without discernment can make you vulnerable to emotional debt—to confusing compassion with compliance, and grace with silence. This chapter delves into the tension between gratitude and resentment, posing the question: *How do you honor what was good without denying what was harmful?* It unpacks how distorted gratitude—rooted in obligation, guilt, or performance—can quietly turn appreciation into self-erasure.

Client Story: The Great Aunt's Question

One of my clients shared that for years her great-aunt has asked the same question at every monthly visit, sometimes directly and sometimes subtly: "When are you going to have children?" She'd told her aunt countless times that she didn't want children. Yet, she continued asking the question at every get-together, even after my client had a partial hysterectomy. Her aunt knew about the surgery. Still, she persisted, as if she couldn't be fulfilled until she got the answer she craved.

To the aunt, those questions came from love, from tradition, from an era that equated womanhood with motherhood. But to my client, they landed like stones—small, repeated reminders that her choices and her reality were not only being dismissed but judged as less than. Her aunt's *intent* was affection. Her *impact* felt like pressure, sounded like criticism, and made her believe she wasn't enough on her own. She shared a very insightful moment:

"It's funny, like everyone else, I came into this world alone, with a celebration of joy to mark my arrival. Yet somewhere along the way, being alone, being just me, stopped being enough."

Her story is a lesson in how easily love, when filtered through control or nostalgia, can wound instead of nurture. Good intentions don't cancel out harm. Gratitude doesn't mean staying silent about pain. Clarity teaches us to hold both truths: *You meant well—and it still hurt.*

The Guilt of Growth

Growth is rarely a clean break from who you were. It's often messy, layered, and full of contradictions—especially when you were conditioned to see shrinking as loyalty. When you start to expand, ask for more, or live beyond the roles you were assigned, it can feel like betrayal. Not because you've done anything wrong, but because the people who benefited from your smallness might see your growth as a rejection of them.

The applause you once received for functioning on little—whether in resources, attention, or care—begins to fade the moment you seek more than merely getting by. And if you've been praised for being "strong" and "grateful" in the face of scarcity, your desire for change can spark a deep inner conflict. This conflict may whisper:

"Who do you think you are? After all they've done for you, you ought to feel grateful."

But here's the truth: authentic gratitude doesn't mean you have to keep living in situations that harm you. It can acknowledge the positives while still making room for grieving what you never had. You can step confidently into the present by refusing to stay attached to the patterns of the past.

Part of this work involves learning to name the guilt you're feeling.

- **The guilt that belongs to you** → The kind that arises when your actions truly cause harm or conflict with your values. It serves as a signal to reflect, repair, and grow.
- **The guilt that isn't yours** → The kind that appears when you've done nothing wrong, but you've been conditioned to feel responsible for others' comfort and happiness.
- **The guilt that stems from empathy** → The feeling that arises when you see someone struggling and wish you could do more, but realize that doing so might drain you, enable them, or keep you stuck in an unhealthy dynamic.
- **The guilt from pushing beyond your limits** → stems from the pressure to do more than you want, can, or should. This often turns the drive to "do it all" into perfectionism, leaving you exhausted, disappointed, and resentful.

- **The guilt that exists only in your mind** → It comes from expecting judgment, rejection, or disapproval that hasn't happened—and might never occur. Instead of facing reality, you're preparing for a possibility, carrying a weight that doesn't yet exist.

When guilt—especially the imagined or exaggerated kind—guides your actions, it becomes a hidden form of self-sabotage. You over-commit. You stretch yourself too thin trying to be the solution to every problem, as if being anything less would make you unworthy. One of the most freeing realizations that clarity brings is understanding that you can feel guilt without being guilty. The feeling may be real, but the verdict isn't always true. Recognizing the difference allows you to stop performing for acceptance and start living in alignment. Where gratitude is genuine and resentment no longer needs to build up in silence.

* * *

Weaponized Gratitude

Sometimes guilt doesn't just live inside you—it's handed to you, wrapped in the words: "You should be grateful." Weaponized gratitude takes something sacred—a value meant to connect—and twists it into a leash. It turns thankfulness into a tool for control, keeping you small, silent, and indebted. It can sound like:

- "You have no idea how good you have it."
- "Other people would kill to be in your position."
- "If it weren't for me, you wouldn't be where you are."

On the surface, these words might sound harmless—or even true. But beneath them lies the real message: *Don't ask for more. Don't name the gaps. Don't make me uncomfortable by telling the truth.* When gratitude is weaponized, it stops being about appreciation and starts being about **appeasement.** You don't say "thank you" because you feel it—you say it because not saying it could cost you: criticism, withdrawal, or conflict. Over time, gratitude becomes performance—smiling through discomfort, swallowing your needs, and downplaying your pain.

Every time you do this, resentment grows. The damage runs deep. **Genuine gratitude builds trust. Weaponized gratitude breeds fear.**

Responding to Weaponized Gratitude

The first step is noticing the difference. Ask yourself:

- Am I expressing thanks because I genuinely feel it—or because I feel like I owe it?
- Is gratitude being used to connect—or to control?

When you respond, you don't have to fight, justify, or overexplain. Calm truth is enough:

- "I appreciate what you did, and there were also parts that were difficult for me."
- "I can be grateful and still be honest about what I need."
- "Can you help me understand what you want me to take away from this?"

Not everyone will welcome your honesty. Some may deflect, minimize, or guilt-trip. Others may surprise you with openness. But the goal isn't to control their reaction—it's to **protect your peace.**

Responding to weaponized gratitude isn't about winning an argument; it's about reclaiming your freedom. **Gratitude should be a gift you give, not a cage you're kept in.**

* * *

Healthy gratitude is honest. It acknowledges the value of what you received while still naming the cost. It makes room for both appreciation and truth—not as opposites, but as partners in understanding. You can be grateful for what helped you without excusing what harmed you, and that balance is where peace begins.

Clarity teaches you not to see things in black and white. Experiences rarely fit neatly into "all good" or "all bad." That kind of thinking clouds discernment. True clarity doesn't mean swapping one extreme for another—it means holding both truths at once. That balance is what allows bitterness and resentment to fade.

However, when gratitude is distorted, it ceases to be a genuine expression of freedom and becomes performance. It shifts from honesty to obligation, from acknowledgment to appeasement. And when you rehearse that script long enough, gratitude stops being your truth and starts serving someone else's comfort.

Here's what performing gratitude looks like:

1. **The Social Script:** Saying "I'm so blessed!" or "I'm grateful for everything" because it's expected—not because it's true. Gratitude becomes a mask for humility, likability, or spiritual maturity.
2. **The Avoidance Tool:** Using gratitude to sidestep pain or injustice. Saying "At least I have a job" to avoid confronting a toxic workplace. Gratitude becomes denial disguised as perspective.
3. **The Guilt Response:** Smiling through dissatisfaction because others "have it worse." Gratitude becomes the excuse to silence your own needs so you don't seem unappreciative.
4. **The Relationship Currency:** Over-thanking to maintain favor, peace, or access to someone's resources. Gratitude becomes transactional—like paying taxes in emotional currency.

Healthy Gratitude Versus Performed Gratitude

Let's lay it out side by side so you can see the difference:

Healthy Gratitude	Performed Gratitude
• Rooted in genuine appreciation.	• Driven by expectation, guilt, or pressure.
• Honest about what was given and why.	• Skips harm, rewrites stories, avoids conflict.
• Leaves you lighter and seen.	• Leaves you small, indebted, and resentful.
• Builds mutual respect.	• Keeps unhealthy dynamics alive.
• Can coexist with boundaries.	• Demands silence to survive.

When you see the difference this clearly, you stop confusing gratitude with compliance. You reclaim the right to tell the truth—even while saying "thank you."

Quick Reflection: Think of a moment in the past month when you said "thank you." Was it because you truly felt grateful—or because you thought you *should*? Did it free you, or keep you small?

* * *

Finding the Balance Between Gratitude and Truth

Gratitude without truth becomes a mask. Truth without gratitude can harden into bitterness. The goal isn't to pick one over the other—it's to let them work together. When gratitude is genuine, it doesn't erase pain; it acknowledges what was good while still naming what was harmful. Recognizing truth doesn't drown you in resentment; it simply names what happened without letting it define your entire identity.

Balance sounds like this:

- "I appreciate what I learned, but I won't excuse the harm that came with it."
- "I can acknowledge their effort, without pretending their impact was harmless."
- "I can be grateful for what I received, while being truthful about what it cost me."

This balance keeps gratitude from collapsing into performance and truth from collapsing into bitterness. Together, they create peace—not the fragile peace of silence, but the grounded peace of alignment.

When Gratitude Turns to Resentment

Resentment often begins in silence. It's the tension you carry when you've been told to *"just be thankful"*—even when the cost you paid was high. At first, you convince yourself you're fine. You smile. You say the right things. You even rehearse your blessings to drown out the discomfort. But the unspoken truth doesn't disappear; it compounds. Every time you hide your pain to protect someone else's comfort, you deplete your emotional reserves. Eventually, you'll have nothing left to give.

Resentment doesn't come from ingratitude—it comes from **imbalance.** It grows when the scales between what you've given and what you've received stay tilted too far for too long. Clarity doesn't require you to release your gratitude; it simply asks you to let it stand beside your honesty. You can be grateful for what you've learned and still acknowledge what it cost. When you do that, resentment loses its grip—because it can only thrive where truth is buried.

From Resentment to Victim Mindset

If resentment lingers too long, it begins to evolve into a victim mindset. That mindset doesn't just *remember* pain—it clings to it, rehearses it, and starts to wear it as identity. Instead of saying, "This hurt me," it begins to whisper, "This is who I am now." In that space, resentment convinces you that joy is betrayal, that healing is pretense, and that moving forward means abandoning your truth. But healing doesn't erase what you endured—it repositions it.

You are not defined by the bed you were forced to lie in. When the invitation to rise appears, it isn't dismissing your pain—it's reminding you that you were never meant to stay pinned to it. Gratitude reminds you that resilience has already carried you further than you imagined. Resentment reminds you of what it cost.

The victim mindset tries to convince you that the cost is your permanent address—like a bill that keeps arriving every month, demanding a payment you'll never be able to make. It tells you that moving forward means forgetting what happened. In reality, healing isn't ignoring the bill—it's **closing the account.**

How Resentment Shows Up

Resentment doesn't always arrive loudly—it often slips in quietly, disguised as composure. It hides behind "I'm fine" or "It's no big deal." But beneath the calm surface, something starts to corrode.

Here are some of the ways it tends to appear:

- **The Distant Helper:** You still show up for people, but your presence feels mechanical. You're doing the bare minimum because the joy of giving has been replaced with obligation (*see Chapter 1: Guarded Giving*).

- **The Hidden Scorecard:** You keep quiet tallies of favors given versus favors returned—not because you want payback, but because you're tired of being the only one keeping score.
- **The Emotional Eye Roll:** You nod, smile, and say "thank you," but inside you're rolling your eyes because the praise feels hollow or manipulative.
- **The Avoidance Pattern:** You start dodging conversations, invitations, or specific people because you no longer trust yourself to stay silent—and you can't keep pretending nothing's wrong.
- **The Sudden Eruption:** After months or years of holding back, one minor incident triggers a reaction that feels "too big." It's not the event itself—it's the release of everything you've suppressed.

Releasing Resentment

Resentment often grows in the shadows of unspoken truths. It thrives where gratitude is demanded, but your pain goes unacknowledged. Holding onto resentment for too long traps you in an emotional cycle—constantly reliving the injustice rather than letting it go. Letting go doesn't mean excusing or forgetting what happened; it means refusing to let it dictate your peace.

Release isn't denial—it's a **reallocation of power.** It's taking energy from what hurts you and reinvesting it in what can grow you. Releasing resentment isn't about pretending the wound didn't happen—it's about deciding that your healing deserves more space than your history.

Insight as a Release Valve

Resentment can consume your thoughts, rob you of peace, and stifle your joy. Left unchecked, it multiplies—feeding on the silence where truth should live. But insight can temper that anger. Insight doesn't excuse harm, but it does explain context. It lets you look beneath the surface—to see the wounds, blind spots, or limitations that shaped someone's choices. Sometimes, that perspective is enough to loosen the grip of resentment. Not because the harm disappears, but because you no longer carry it in the same way.

Insight allows you to say, "I see why you acted that way, even if it still hurts me." That kind of clarity can be freeing. Because sometimes what brings release is not the apology you're still waiting on—but the perspective that allows you to stop rehearsing the injustice on repeat. Clarity reframes resentment into something livable: not a permanent wound, but a scar with meaning.

Resentment is often the waiting room of forgiveness. You sit with the ache, the imbalance, the endless replay of what should have been different—hoping something will make it lighter. But clarity reminds you: forgiveness isn't forgetting, and it isn't reconciliation. It's simply choosing not to let resentment dictate your emotional reality anymore. Letting go doesn't erase the cost—it releases you from paying it every single day. We'll go deeper into forgiveness in Chapter 11. For now, remember this: when you begin to loosen resentment's grip, you're giving *yourself*—not them—the gift of peace.

The Rope of Resentment

I once heard a great analogy: Resentment is like gripping a rope that ties you to what's behind you. The longer you hold on, the more it burns your hands. The heavier it gets, the more it pulls your gaze backward. Letting go of the rope doesn't mean pretending the past didn't happen—it means you stop letting it drag you into yesterday. Insight loosens the knot. Forgiveness cuts the cord. And clarity gives you the courage to unclench your grip, finally. Only then are you free to face a future that isn't chained to your past.

Acceptance

Acceptance isn't about tying everything up neatly or pretending you're at peace before you really are. It's about acknowledging reality—without resistance, justification, or denial. It's saying, "This happened. I may not like it. I may not understand it. But I no longer want it to own me." Acceptance doesn't rush you toward forgiveness or demand that you feel grateful before you're ready. It's quieter than that—more about posture than progress. It's the internal stance, not necessarily the outward proof, that you have stopped fighting the truth of what was and are willing to find steadiness in what is.

It can look like:

- Writing what you wish you could say, even if you never send it.
- Taking small, intentional steps that honor your turning point—like releasing what no longer serves you, revisiting a memory with new eyes, or creating a quiet routine to mark your shift from resistance to peace.
- Letting unanswered questions exist without letting them dictate your peace.

The purpose of acceptance isn't to erase the past—it's to stop resisting it. It makes space for healing to grow, for gratitude to become genuine, and for peace to feel possible again. Acceptance doesn't depend on anyone else changing, apologizing, or seeing your side of things. In fact, it begins the moment you stop waiting for them to.

And here's where clarity reshapes everything: acceptance doesn't mean agreement, forgiveness, or indifference. It means you've stopped rehearsing *what should have been* and started living in *what is*. Forgiveness may come later (we'll go deeper in Chapter 11), but acceptance steadies you *here and now*. It doesn't erase the complexity of your story—it gives it room to breathe. Because sometimes, the people who hurt you were also trying to help. And that tension—

between their intention and their impact—is where understanding begins, and resentment begins to loosen its hold.

* * *

Good Intentions ≠ Good Impact

One of the most brutal truths to face is this: someone can love you, mean well, and still cause harm. Intent doesn't erase impact. It may be true that they were "doing their best," but their best was shaped by their own wounds, blind spots, or fears. Maybe they acted from anxiety instead of wisdom, control instead of care. And while understanding where they came from might soften your anger, it doesn't erase your right to grieve, protect yourself, or expect better. Think of it this way: if someone steps on your foot, it hurts whether they did it by accident or on purpose. You can determine that it wasn't malicious and still expect them to move off your foot. Intent explains the action—but it doesn't erase the bruise.

When we cling to the belief that good intentions guarantee good outcomes, we excuse harm. We rationalize behavior because we fear seeming ungrateful, disloyal, or "too sensitive." But compassion isn't the same as continued access, and forgiveness isn't the same as permission. Clarity calls you to hold both truths at once: *Yes, you meant well. And yes, I was still hurt.* That dual awareness keeps you from collapsing into bitterness on one side or blind loyalty on the other.

Examples of "Good Intentions" That Still Cause Harm

- A parent urging choices that mirror their own story—less to prepare you for life, more to preserve the version of it they wanted for themselves.

- A friend hiding the truth "to spare you"—only to blindside you later.
- A boss piling on tasks "because you're capable"—rewarding competence with burnout.

Forgiveness Versus Permission

Forgiveness releases the grip pain has on you. Permission hands that pain the key to your peace. You can forgive without allowing someone to return to a role where they repeatedly break trust.

Compassion Versus Continued Access

Compassion says, "I understand your struggle." Continued access says, "I'll keep letting you hurt me." The first reflects your humanity. The second endangers your peace. Clarity teaches this simple truth: good intentions may explain behavior, but they don't excuse harm. Love without accountability becomes enabling. Care without respect becomes control. Meaning well is not the same as *doing* well. And if you've been harmed, you are allowed to protect your peace—without apology.

Even when the harm isn't malicious, it often leaves behind an invisible residue—a quiet sense of debt. You start to believe that because someone *meant well* or *helped you once*, you now owe them your silence, your compliance, or your continued loyalty. That's where good intentions turn into emotional accounting—and where gratitude becomes currency instead of connection. And that's where the next layer of clarity begins: **unlearning the debt mentality**—the belief that appreciation must come at the cost of autonomy because freedom loses its meaning when you feel indebted for being helped.

* * *

Unlearning the Debt Mentality

Many of us learn—directly or indirectly—that love, support, or opportunity often come with strings attached. Maybe those strings are subtle, like a "Don't forget who helped you" comment. Or perhaps they're woven into your family, cultural, or faith storylines: *You owe your parents unquestioning loyalty. You owe your mentor your obedience. You owe the community your silence.*

This is the **debt mentality**—the belief that when someone gives, you must repay them with your compliance, availability, or even your self-betrayal. It turns care into a contract you never agreed to, trapping gratitude in an endless loop of "paying back" instead of moving forward. Debt-based gratitude often sounds like:

- *I can't refuse—they've done so much for me.*
- *They gave me this chance, so I can't speak up about what's wrong.*
- *I should be grateful that they even chose me, so I won't ask for more.*

The problem? This kind of "repayment" is rarely about the present moment. It's about maintaining an emotional balance sheet for life. You don't just thank them once; you repay the favor with your time, silence, and energy long after the original gift.

Breaking the Cycle

Unlearning the debt mentality means separating **gratitude** from **obligation**. You can value what someone gave you without letting it control your choices today. You can recognize their role in your past without letting it dictate your future. It looks like this:

- Saying "thank you" without also saying "yes" to harm.
- Letting a gift remain a gift—not a lifetime subscription to your loyalty.

- Remembering that moving forward doesn't always mean leaving others behind.

When you let go of debt-based gratitude, you create space for relationships built on mutual respect—free from emotional IOUs. You regain the freedom to evolve beyond the version of yourself that someone once helped shape, without guilt that your growth is betrayal.

Quick Reflection: Are You Holding Emotional Debt?

Grab a notebook and reflect:

- **The "Owe You" List:** Who do you feel indebted to because of what they once gave, did, or said?
- **The Hidden Costs:** What is that "debt" costing you now—time, peace, or freedom?
- **Gift or Contract?** Was what they gave truly a gift—or did it come with an expectation attached?
- **Releasing the Tab:** Where could you thank someone for what they gave, while letting go of the ongoing obligation?

Note: You don't have to confront anyone to close the account. Sometimes, releasing emotional debt starts with allowing yourself.

🔄 Reframe: Clarity as Emotional Freedom

Clarity teaches you this: gratitude should never feel like a leash. True thankfulness doesn't bind you to harmful patterns or keep you indebted to people who "meant well" but missed the mark. Authentic gratitude is a choice, not a chain—something you can carry without bending under its weight.

When you stop seeking belongingness as a form of repayment and begin practicing gratitude from a genuine conviction, you reclaim your freedom. Freedom to acknowledge what was good without denying what was costly. Freedom to say "thank you" without saying "I owe you."

And that's the freedom this chapter has been leading you toward: gratitude that feels like choice, not debt—peace that doesn't require pretending, and clarity that refuses to confuse thankfulness with docility.

* * *

🌙 Emotional Arc – Chapter 6: Gratitude and Resentment

Core Tension

You were taught to show gratitude regardless of the cost—to smile through disappointment, minimize harm, and measure your worth by how well you could "take it." Questioning what you were given made you seem ungrateful; naming harm felt like betrayal. But suppressing truth only bred resentment.

Positive Balance

Clarity shows that gratitude and truth can coexist. You can honor what helped you without excusing what hurt you. You can value effort without pretending the impact was harmless. This balance turns gratitude from a mask you wear into an anchor you hold—grounded in reality, rooted in self-respect.

Empowering Tone

You no longer need to choose between honesty and grace. You can speak truth without bitterness, release resentment without rewriting history, and let gratitude stand beside truth—not in place of it.

When gratitude is rooted in reality, it becomes steady—not a performance, not a debt, not a prison. This is emotional freedom—and it's yours to protect.

* * *

Chapter 6 Summary and Closing: Gratitude and Resentment

Chapter 6 reminded you that gratitude should set you free, not imprison you. That resentment isn't the opposite of thankfulness, but a result of silence and tolerating harm without limits. It showed you that you can hold gratitude and truth together, sincerely. You recognized where gratitude shifts into performance, obligation, or emotional currency. You saw resentment not as a sign of ingratitude but as proof of truths long buried. You distinguished between healthy gratitude that frees you and false gratitude that constrains you.

Clarity provided a new perspective: gratitude isn't about ignoring pain or excusing harm at your own expense. It's about acknowledging the whole picture—joy and grief, release and remembrance—and still choosing a path that doesn't sacrifice your happiness.

Practicing gratitude this way isn't fragile or forced. It allows space for grief without guilt, lessons without lingering bitterness, and hope without pretending the hurt never happened. It's less about "what you should feel" and more about honoring what is true. Because gratitude isn't just a feeling, it's a choice—and when it's chosen honestly, it becomes freedom you can actually live in.

✦ Chapter 6: Gratitude and Resentment – Pause for Perspective

Virtue: Contentment

Contentment isn't the absence of desire—it's the ability to hold desire and peace in the same breath. It's not about lowering your standards or pretending you're satisfied when you're not. It's a conscious choice to fully embrace the season you're in—without letting what you've lost or what you still long for steal the joy available to you now.

True contentment is not something that comes naturally to most people. There is a special "secret" needed to learn how to be content no matter your situation. What is that secret? Developing specific virtues, many of which have already been identified in this chapter and book. What are some main ones to focus on? Gratitude, humility, and hope. Cultivating these qualities will help you to view your situation from a different perspective.

Contentment doesn't eliminate pain, grief, or longing, nor should it eliminate the setting of realistic goals. Instead, it allows you to hold them without being overwhelmed. It's the steady middle ground where gratitude and truth meet—where you can honor the good without denying the harm, and release what you can't change without giving up on what's still possible. In practice, contentment looks like:

- Appreciating what shaped you without being bound to what broke you.
- Acknowledging pain without letting it become your whole story.
- Using humility to redefine what true success means.
- Allowing joy, even in small moments, to coexist with disappointment.
- Refusing to postpone peace until life feels "perfect."

Clarity shows that contentment is not complacency—it's resilience. It's the quiet strength to say:

- *Gratitude will prevent my history from holding me hostage.*
- *Humility won't allow my present to swallow me whole.*
- *My future is still unfolding, and I can carry joy, peace, and hope with me on my journey.*

If this chapter helped you see your past and present through a more empowering lens of gratitude, the next step is to examine how that old perspective has shaped how you've been showing up. When gratitude was rooted in survival, connection often became performance—and it's time to untangle the two.

☞ Next Steps: Workbook Journal Prompts

For a deeper look at how gratitude, truth, and contentment can transform your relationships, decisions, and inner peace, refer to the companion workbook for Chapter 6.

 ## Personal Notes & Insights

Use this page to capture any quotes, ideas, or personal revelations that surfaced while reading. Let it be messy, real, and yours.

_____

_____

_____

_____

_____

_____

_____

_____

_____

_____

_____

_____

_____

_____

_____

TO THE ONE I HAD TO STOP PERFORMING FOR

You don't owe anyone the version of yourself that makes you feel empty.

I was assigned a role I never auditioned for. And for years, I gave my best performance. I memorized the script you handed me. I became your pride piece, your proof that your story still worked. But I never felt like I could be both real and loved. When I missed a line, praise turned into punishment. Affection became control. And my body, my voice, my choices—became props in a production I didn't write.

I spent years chasing your standing ovation—keeping the spotlight soft enough not to expose my pain, staying in character even after the story stopped making sense. But I was never yours to direct. You're not my author. I'm not your understudy. My life is my own.

I no longer crave your applause to feel valuable. I no longer mistake silence for peace or control for love. I no longer confuse performance with connection. You may never understand what this role cost me—but I do. And that knowing is my closure.

With clarity,
Shante

CHAPTER 7
PERFORMATIVE CONNECTION

Clarity not only exposes the mask, but it also reveals who you truly were beneath it all along.

Chapter 7 picks up where Chapter 6 left off—with truth no longer masked for the sake of being pleasing. Gratitude helped you recognize what shaped you. Now, clarity asks you to face what you've been acting out. Many of us were taught to stay connected by remaining "in character." We learned to preserve relationships by adopting roles—the strong one, the fixer, the shining star, the invisible shadow. Beneath each performance was the quiet hope of being seen.

This chapter isn't about who you had to be for them. It's about who you must stop being to become yourself, finally. Performance may have earned proximity, but it never gave you intimacy. This is where the performance ends—where the "go-to," the "one who never drops the ball," the "always reliable" finally puts the script down. Here, sincerity replaces strategy. This is where you stop performing and start becoming.

🎭 The Roles We Learn to Play

Sometimes the mask isn't just something you wear—it's something you're handed. You didn't choose it; you were often selected because of it. High achievers often get cast into roles because they're competent, composed, and self-sufficient. But those same qualities can become cages when your worth is only recognized through performance.

Before you can put down the script, you have to name the role. These aren't just habits—they're masks. Masks we wear to maintain proximity, to stay liked, to feel safe. You become:

- **The Strong One** – Carries the weight for everyone, never wavering.
- **The Fixer** – Solves problems (even unspoken ones) to preserve peace or control.
- **The Shining Star** – Performs, achieves, excels—to stay admired and validated.
- **The Invisible Shadow** – Blends in, avoids conflict, suppresses needs.
- **The Entertainer** – Uses humor or charm to soften pain and tension.
- **The Go-To** – Always reliable, accessible, self-sacrificing—even when it hurts.

These roles weren't random—they were rewarded. You were praised for being agreeable, adaptable, or invisible. Over time, that praise replaced your voice. You smiled under pressure, nodded to dismissal, and stayed silent amid violation. Not because you lacked depth, but because you were celebrated for disappearing. Eventually, those roles became armor—and sometimes identity. But the longer you perform the part, the harder it becomes to tell:

Is this who I am—or who I had to become to stay safe, needed, and accepted?

Clarity disrupts the role. It exposes the cost of your mask. And it demands something radical in return: authenticity over approval. Authenticity has no role to play. It doesn't audition or perform—it just is. That's why it feels risky. Because when you drop the act, you're no longer protected by applause. You're visible. Unmasked. Human.

The Performance of Connection: Staying Liked by Remaining in Character

Performative connection isn't rooted in who you are—it's built on who you had to hide to stay connected. It thrives on one condition: that you don't get too real. It rewards your mask, not your mind. It praises your presence as long as you don't take up space. It celebrates your loyalty, but only if you stay silent.

We often speak of connection as if it's naturally mutual—honest, sustaining, effortless. But for many of us, our connections were managed, negotiated, or manipulated from the start. You learned that being liked meant being helpful. Being trusted meant being agreeable. Being loved meant being low-maintenance. So, you adjusted. Softened your truth. Refined your performance until connection became choreography—a careful dance to avoid disappointment, conflict, abandonment, or rejection.

Performative connection looks like:

- Smiling through microaggressions to avoid conflict.
- Holding back the truth to protect someone else's comfort.
- Ignoring manipulation to avoid being labeled "the problem."
- Downplaying your emotions so others don't have to face theirs.
- Laughing at jokes that sting to avoid being "too sensitive."
- Over-explaining yourself to avoid being misjudged.

Performative connection is costly. Even when people say they love you, what they often mean is: *I love the version of you that doesn't challenge me.* They love the role you play in their story, not the fullness of who you are. And if you dare to unmask—to speak honestly, to rest, to take up space—you may feel the sting of withdrawal or abandonment. Not because you did something wrong, but because you stopped performing for their comfort.

Clarity makes the mask heavy. It begins with discomfort—a quiet ache of being surrounded but unseen. Useful, but not embraced. Chosen, but not known. Removing the mask is the radical act of refusing to overperform for love you already deserve. It's choosing truth even when the room prefers your edited version. Not everyone will know what to do with your unfiltered presence—but the right ones will. Authenticity may not always bring the most attention, but it brings the most peace.

Performative connection is about safety, not sincerity. But the longer you live in survival mode, the more honesty starts to feel like danger instead of strength. Eventually, you realize: if love requires performance, it's not love—it's an act. When your worth is measured by how much you carry, collapse feels like failure. But that's not a connection. That's survival in costume. And one day, you'll hear the whisper: *You don't have to keep performing like this.* Once you hear that truth, you can't unhear it. That's when you know—you've been cast in a role you never auditioned for. And now, you're ready to walk offstage.

Client Vignette: "The Boardroom Whisper"

I had a client who had mastered her script. Her tone was measured. Her smile was neutral. And her feedback, always diplomatic. Years of experience, two degrees, and a leadership title hadn't freed her; they'd perfected her performance. In meetings, she was "the voice of reason." In evaluations, "the one who keeps everyone calm." But in private, she replayed every conversation, wondering if she had been too direct, too quiet, too much.

When she finally challenged a decision that undermined her team, the room fell silent. Her words were measured, her reasoning sound—but the tension was thick enough to taste. The next day, a senior executive pulled her aside and said, "You're usually so composed. That was . . . unlike you."

Unlike her? Or unlike the version of her they preferred? As she and I discussed this incident, she came to realize that she had never been rewarded for her leadership—only for her compliance. The clarity was sharp and cold: she had spent years earning respect that depended on her silence. So, at the next meeting, she didn't apologize for taking up space. She didn't smooth the edges of truth. She didn't wait to be invited to speak. The discomfort in the room was familiar—but this time, she didn't mistake it for danger. She had finally gone off-script.

* * *

🎭 Poetry Reflection: The Performance Trap
(Inspired by Paul Laurence Dunbar's "We Wear the Mask," 1895—public domain)

> We wear the mask that grins and lies,
> It hides our cheeks and shades our eyes,
> This debt we pay to human guile;
> With torn and bleeding hearts we smile . . .

I first heard "We Wear the Mask" at the age of 11 on the show *A Different World*, and I can still recite those first four lines from memory. As a little Black girl, I didn't need anyone to explain it—I understood it in my bones. Those words felt like they belonged to me, my parents, my siblings, my extended family, and my friends. One way or another, we were all smiling through exhaustion.

Now, as an adult, I know its reach is far greater. Dunbar's poem reveals a truth that transcends race, gender, and generation: we all wear masks to survive. I've seen it as a coach, walking with hundreds of people from every background imaginable. The truth is universal: we're tired. Tired of performing counterfeit success. Tired of proving competence. Tired of pretending that composure means peace—of confusing holding it together with being whole.

The poem reminds us that the mask is something society applauds—the polished smile, the efficient worker, the dependable friend—while quietly ignoring the cost beneath. We tell ourselves the road of achievement is paved with fulfillment, but too often it's layered with quiet disconnection, invisible pressure, and the ache of pretending to be "fine."

But here's the hope: clarity offers a choice. You can decide when and where to lay the mask down. You can build a life that doesn't require performance as a form of protection. A path where authenticity doesn't endanger you—it frees you. Remove the mask. Breathe. Be seen. The world may not always honor your reality, but you can.

But taking off the mask doesn't end the performance overnight—it exposes the cost of going off-script. Because once you stop pretending, you start noticing who was only clapping for the act.

* * *

The Cost of Going Off-Script

There's a kind of connection that feels like a script—the lines unspoken but well-rehearsed. You know your cues:

- Keep it simple. Don't ask for much.
- Don't challenge their version of reality.
- Protect their image. Silence your truth. Maintain harmony.

But what happens when the script no longer fits—when clarity makes it impossible to keep going? You start to notice things: the tone shifts, warmth cools, praise turns into pressure, and attention becomes control. The connection feels less like care and more like a transaction. Because you were never chosen for who you are—only for how you serve. And the moment you step out of character, the consequences arrive quickly:

- Guilt.
- Silence.
- Condemnation.
- Distance.
- Retaliation.
- Labels: "difficult," "disloyal," "ungrateful."

You realize truth often feels like betrayal to those whose loyalty depended on your silence.

The Danger of Dropping the Mask

Not everyone is offended by your flaws—some are offended by your freedom. Especially when that freedom lets you name what no longer feels right. When you drop the mask, you interrupt the illusion. You expose the performance for what it is: practiced closeness without real intimacy. There's grief in that realization. Because the role you played so well wasn't love—it was survival.

In Personal Spaces, Going Off-Script Might Look Like

- Naming harm within a family that values appearances
- Redefining loyalty instead of obeying it
- Refusing to laugh at hurtful jokes
- Breaking generational rules you were never allowed to question
- Admitting exhaustion instead of pretending to be strong
- Speaking truth and watching the room turn cold

Telling the truth might get you branded "the problem" or "the black sheep." But often, being called the black sheep only means you were the first to stop pretending.

In Professional Spaces, Going Off-Script Might Look Like

- Not answering after-hours messages
- Declining the promotion that costs your peace
- Stepping off a leadership path you never chose
- Naming dysfunction in a culture that rewards silence
- Saying "I'm at capacity" instead of taking on more
- Choosing truth over teamwork when teamwork becomes complicity

When you're competent—the one everyone depends on—it's even harder. They may praise your composure, but their reactions often reveal the truth: **We'll value you as long as you stay compliant, absorb our pace, and never disrupt the story we tell about ourselves—or the role we've assigned to you.**

What Happens When You Refuse the Script

You're branded disruptive, defiant, disloyal. Not because you failed—but because you stopped betraying yourself to maintain a false peace. When the curtain falls, a deeper question emerges—one clarity won't let you outrun: *Who are you when you're no longer performing?*

Truth: Improvising Exposes the Entire Performance

When you stop performing, you finally see behind the curtain. You notice who only clapped when you delivered the right lines—and who never really saw you at all. That's when the grief comes: realizing the connection you fought to preserve wasn't real. It was built on your silence. But here's the gift:

- You can stop curating yourself to feel safe.
- Stop performing strength when what you need is rest.
- Stop calling survival love.
- Belonging doesn't require self-abandonment.

You're free to write new stories—ones where honesty doesn't make you disposable, and being genuine doesn't cost your security. Going off-script doesn't ruin the story; it marks the moment you became the author.

It's where eye-service ends and integrity begins—where connection is built through congruence, not compliance, and your outer life finally matches your inner truth. There's something magnetic about those who no longer posture. They don't edit their presence to earn a sense of belonging. They are. Their genuineness isn't loud—it's unforgettable.

* * *

Over-functioning Often Seems Like Strength—Until It Doesn't

Some people perform to be liked. Others perform to survive. But high achievers? We perform because excellence has become our identity—the version of ourselves that always gets rewarded. We were praised for being reliable, driven, gifted—and we believed it, because it was true. But no one warned us that being exceptional could become a trap. Once we became "the one who gets things done," people stopped asking what it was costing us.

You become the one who keeps everything running. You step in when others fall short, solve problems, fill gaps, and pick up what others drop. Because you do it so well, no one thinks to ask if you *need* help. And if they do, you likely decline it. Over time, competence becomes captivity. The more you carry, the less anyone notices the weight. The more invisible your effort becomes, the harder you push—to prove you still matter.

When Strengths Become a Script

High performers often focus on achieving without pausing to reflect on their progress. But before you chase the next breakthrough, I want you to know—there's another way. One of the most precise and compassionate tools I've used to help clients reconnect with their natural wiring after years of overdoing or self-abandonment is the **CliftonStrengths® assessment**.

It's not just about *what* you do well—it's about *how* you do it: how you build relationships, process information, and make things happen. More importantly, it reveals where your strengths might become overextensions when you're disconnected from rest, authenticity, or emotional connection.

You can take the official assessment at gallup.com/cliftonstrengths. Before we continue: the reflections that follow are based on the CliftonStrengths framework developed by Gallup, but the blindspot insights are my own—shaped by years of coaching high achievers as a Gallup-Certified Strengths Coach. Sometimes your greatest strengths reinforce the very roles you're trying to outgrow.

- **Responsibility, Achiever, Maximizer:** Drive you to excel—but when unchecked, they become internal scorecards measuring your worth by output and consistency.
- **Significance:** Keeps you visible, but can make you fear losing respect if you stop overdelivering.
- **Individualization:** Tunes you so deeply into others that you lose connection with yourself.
- **Harmony and Empathy:** Beautiful in balance, but when overused, they silence hard truths to preserve comfort.

Strategic thinkers can overanalyze their next move, thereby avoiding emotional clarity. **Restorative** types may fix everything and everyone, mistaking control for care. And **Competition**, when driven by comparison rather than growth, can turn success into silent burnout disguised as ambition.

Your strengths aren't flaws—but when fueled by fear, pressure, or identity, they intensify performance rather than break its cycle. Even once you understand your strengths, another truth remains: many of us grew up only being loved for the versions of ourselves that achieved, pleased, or performed. When love feels earned through performance, authenticity starts to feel like rebellion.

Strengths in Overdrive: A Self-Reflection Check-In

Your greatest strengths can become heavy burdens when fueled by fear, guilt, or the need to prove yourself. Sometimes, our strengths become masks—we over-rely on them not just to succeed, but to *survive*. Pause and consider:

- Which strengths do I lean on most when I feel anxious, guilty, or unseen?
- When I overwork, what strength might I be overusing to avoid vulnerability or rest?
- Do I use specific strengths to keep others happy—or to stay invisible?
- Am I afraid that if I stop overdelivering, I'll lose respect or relevance?
- Have any of my strengths become conditions for feeling worthy?
- **Complete this sentence:** "I thought I was being [*strong trait*], but I was really avoiding [*hard truth or unmet need*]."

Your strengths are not the problem. But when they become armor, autopilot, or identity, they can drain you as fast as they once fueled you. Now that you've explored where your strengths might be overextended, let's name what that costs—because the price of over-functioning isn't just physical. It's deeply emotional.

* * *

🎨 Art Reflection: Blue Monday (Annie Lee, 1985)

When I was growing up, my mother had a framed print of *Blue Monday* by Annie Lee hanging above her bed. She told me that every morning, she sat just like that woman—shoulders bent forward, palms resting on her knees, staring into the quiet before the next long day began. At about ten years old, I understood it—without her having to explain it. That's why it stayed with me all these years. I could relate to it in some unspoken way. It looked like stress, burnout, and unmanaged boundaries—on its way to breakdown. It was the image of someone carrying everything and allowed to rest nowhere, even while in her bed.

This painting was done in 1985. Nearly forty years later, has anything really changed? Most would say it's gotten worse. With technology, the expectation isn't just to do more—but to look flawless while doing it. The only thing that's increased since Lee painted *Blue Monday* is burnout—especially among women who've learned to make survival look empowering.

Now I understand why it drew my mother in. For so many women—especially those who hold families, careers, and expectations together with an invisible thread—*Blue Monday* isn't just a painting. It's a mirror. It reflects what it means to wake up to the weight of being "the one who gets it done."

The color blue, often associated with melancholy, also represents devotion and endurance—a love that keeps showing up. But endurance without replenishment becomes emptiness. That's the cost of overfunctioning: appearing composed while quietly collapsing.

Pause here. Take one deep breath. Think of every woman, every leader, every giver who has ever woken up like that—and then remember: you don't have to sit there forever.

* * *

Emotions Connected to Excessive Responsibility

You may look strong on the outside—but inside, the weight of being the reliable one, the fixer, the achiever, the "go-to," takes its toll. When responsibility becomes a reflex instead of a choice, even your strengths start to betray you. Over time, what once made you proud becomes what makes you tired. And the emotions you've buried to keep showing up start to surface. This next section doesn't just name those feelings—it honors them so you can choose to move with more intentionality.

1. **Resentment:** At the heart of hyper-responsibility grows resentment—the quiet ache of feeling unappreciated. You keep saying yes, but inside, you're shouting for someone to see that you're drowning.
2. **Guilt:** You feel guilty for wanting rest, for saying no, for dropping the ball—even when it was never yours to carry. Guilt becomes the leash that pulls you back into roles that drain you.
3. **Anxiety:** The pressure of being the one who "gets it done" keeps you in a constant state of alertness. You're always watching for the next emergency, fearing that if you don't step in, everything will fall apart.
4. **Shame:** You feel ashamed when you can't keep up—when your body fails, when you forget something, or when you

don't want to keep performing. You associate struggling with failing.

5. **Anger:** It simmers. Sometimes silently, sometimes not. You're angry that others don't step up and that you are invisible because help is never offered. But often, the anger turns inward before it's ever expressed.
6. **Loneliness:** You begin to believe that no one else can—or will—share the burden with you. Your worth is often tied to your usefulness. And when you're not being helpful, you feel profoundly alone.
7. **Bitterness:** After years of giving, giving, giving, you begin to feel bitter, not just toward others, but toward yourself for allowing the very patterns that are now eroding your confidence.
8. **Exhaustion:** Hyper-responsibility isn't just exhausting; it's draining. You can't remember the last time you did something simply because you wanted to, not because you had to carry the burden.

* * *

Saying Yes to Roles You Never Asked For

As a high achiever, leadership often identifies you before you even raise your hand. You're handed complex projects without consent, praised for potential that carries unspoken expectations, and nudged into positions you never sought. But being *capable* is not the same as being *called*. You end up climbing ladders that weren't built for your vision—worried that stepping down will make others question your value.

And what's worse? You *deliver*. You exceed expectations. You lead without the title, manage without the authority, and perform without the paycheck. No raise. No recognition. Just a quiet assumption that you'll always rise to the occasion. You become the backbone of teams, initiatives, and entire systems—yet your effort remains invisible because you never made noise about what it cost you. Over time, the gap between what you give and what you get becomes impossible to ignore.

When You Can Do Anything, Who Are You Really?

For multi-talented people, clarity can be especially elusive. You excel in multiple areas. You adapt quickly. You've been praised for being versatile, dependable, and someone who can "figure it out" wherever you go. But what happens when you're skilled in so many things that you don't know which ones are truly yours?

You move from project to project, career to career, identity to identity—driven by confusion, capacity, and sometimes boredom. You say yes because you *can*, not because you've asked yourself if you *should*. And while others see talent and range, you often feel unanchored, scattered, or disconnected from your deeper purpose. This is one of the hidden burdens of competence: the world keeps offering you opportunities, but never teaches you how to discern which ones actually lead back to *yourself*. That's your job now. It's time to define your voice and your values—on purpose.

This is the danger of unexamined strength: when your gifts are used to support everyone else's vision but never your own. Adaptability turns into erasure. Excellence becomes currency. And if you're not careful, even your joy gets commodified. You begin turning every talent into a side hustle, every strength into a service, every interest into income.

Not because you're greedy—but because you've been conditioned to believe that if it isn't productive, it isn't valuable. You start to confuse output with identity. And in the endless cycle of trying to "find yourself through doing," you overlook the quiet clarity that comes from simply being.

Reflection Prompt: When Capability Becomes a Cage

- What parts of your life have been shaped more by *ability* than *alignment*?
- Which roles have you said yes to because of expectation—not desire?
- Where in your life has "'being needed'" been replaced by "'being known'"?
- What strengths or talents have you commodified out of habit or pressure?
- Are you creating a life that reflects your *voice* or your *value* to others?

Take a breath. Write your answers without judgment. This is not about blame—it's about clarity.

* * *

When Thinking Becomes Overburdening

You're not just a doer—you're a thinker, a feeler, a planner, a protector. In your mind, you're carrying backup plans, unspoken worries, emotional tension, and a mental map of everything that could go wrong. You anticipate five steps ahead—not always from simple accomplishment, but from anxiety, fear, or a need to stay in control. And because most of this effort is invisible, no one realizes how overworked your mind really is. The over-analysis, absorption, and mental rehearsal, hyper-vigilance, and silent forecasting—it's not just thinking. It's mental over-functioning. And it's exhausting.

The Inner Critic of the Performer: When Imposter Syndrome Feels Like Truth

Imposter syndrome *is* a performative connection at its core. It thrives in environments where:

- Your worth feels tied to performance or perfection.
- You're praised for a polished version of yourself.
- You fear being "found out" if you stop over-functioning.
- Success feels like a role you're playing—not something you own.

You've been told you're impressive, accomplished, intelligent, and exceptional. But deep down, you're still waiting for someone to call you out—as if none of it is real. As if none of it is enough. What you're battling with isn't humility; it's imposter syndrome. And it's not a sign that you're unqualified. It's a signal that your success has been disconnected from your self-worth. It creeps in when:

- Your accomplishments feel accidental.
- You over-prepare out of fear, not passion.
- You interpret rest as laziness.
- You believe mistakes mean you're not enough.

But here's the truth: You don't have to overperform to deserve the seat you've earned. Clarity reminds you—you belong, even without the performance.

🎭 Dance Reflection: Movements Unseen

When I was a child, the **Dance Theatre of Harlem** was just six blocks away from my home. My best friend had the great fortune of having a godmother who could pay for her to take lessons there. Several times, I walked with her as she entered the building—neatly dressed in her leotard and tights, hair brushed into a perfect bun. I'd linger in the doorway, watching the young dancers practice their positions and steps. I longed to learn, but we couldn't afford the classes. My desire to dance, though, was no secret. I performed African dance in after-school programs and hip-hop at community shows. But modern dance—modern was different. That one I practiced in secret.

It was the one form of expression that was mine, because fear kept it hidden and opportunity kept it out of reach. In my living room, on the rare occasions I had the house to myself, I'd move freely—bare feet sliding across the floor, my body telling stories I didn't yet have the words for. But I never allowed anyone to see me doing it. I was terrified of not being perfect. I knew I didn't have the frame or the figure of the girls who passed through those studio doors, and that thought, strangely, soothed me—it made my absence feel inevitable, not personal.

In forty-five years, I can count only two times I've let someone see me dance like that. Once, as a child, a friend insisted on coming over to watch despite my resistance. The second time, decades later, among a small circle of women I trusted. Both times, the reaction was the same—complete silence. The kind that lingers uncomfortably for too long.

Finally, someone whispered, "That was beautiful." But by then, the silence had already done its work. I mistook it for judgment when it was probably awe. They weren't expecting what I brought into that room. Yet my mind only clung to the seconds that said, *Who do you think you are?* Shame rose before I even knew why. Even now, I feel uneasy acknowledging that I was good—and that the shame still lingers.

I let imposter syndrome convince me that because I hadn't been formally trained, I had no right to call what I did "dance." I let fear dictate that the only parts of myself worth sharing were the ones that others had validated. I wish I could say that once I got older and had the means, I finally took my modern dance class. I didn't, and I haven't. I don't even do it in my own living room anymore; I've limited myself to dancing like that only in my mind.

Now, I am working on applying what clarity has shown me. That living room floor was my first stage. My perfectionism wasn't discipline—it was self-protection. Imposter syndrome stole my joy of movement by ironically turning expression into performance. But clarity invites you back to freedom—to move, to create, to be, without the need for an audience.

Because that's what imposter syndrome does—it tricks you into dismissing anything that isn't public, polished, or praised. That which is private, imperfect, or purely for joy doesn't count. That if no one sees it, it doesn't matter. But the truth is, the unseen expressions are often the most honest ones—it's where the real you lives.

The question clarity whispers next: *Who are you when no one's watching—when you stop performing, stop proving, and simply exist?*

* * *

Clarity Question: Who Are You Without "Doing?"

When your identity is built on being effective, efficient, and exceptional, rest feels like a risk. Slowing down seems selfish. Ease feels like laziness. So, you pour all your energy into one area—usually work, caregiving, or being the family matriarch—while other parts of your life quietly fall into the background. Your joy gets delayed. Your health gets postponed. You become buried under the weight of constant doing. But clarity doesn't shame you for how you've coped. It simply asks:

- *"Is this still working for me?"*
- *Where in my life am I over-preparing, over-functioning, or overthinking out of fear instead of passion?*
- *Which of your accomplishments still feels like a role you're playing rather than something you truly own?*

You are not just the finisher, the fixer, the parent, the partner, the professional. You are someone who deserves support—not just for what you can do, but for who you are. Your exhaustion isn't owed to anyone. Your depletion isn't a badge of honor.

🔁 Reframe: Clarity as Freedom from Performance

- Clarity encourages you to move from auditioning to aligning.
- You don't always need to be agreeable to be accepted.
- You don't have to be impressive to be valued, or excessively adaptable to be loved.
- Your worth isn't measured by how much space you take up—or how little.

When you stop performing to preserve the connection and start practicing presence instead, your relationships begin to shift—from obligation to authenticity. From survival to sincerity. Because genuine connection doesn't require perfection, it isn't about polish—it's about embracing your humanity.

* * *

🌀 Emotional Arc – Chapter 7: Performative Connection

Core Tension

Chapter 7 revealed that not every connection is genuine. A connection built on performance isn't the same as a connection built on presence. You've mastered the art of being *likable*. The version of you that's agreeable, accommodating, and always "on" has been rewarded with access, opportunity, and the illusion of belonging. But the applause isn't for your authentic self—it's for the role you've been playing. And no matter how convincing your performance, you can feel the quiet ache of the disconnect between the mask and the person underneath.

Positive Balance

Clarity reveals that authentic connection isn't something you *earn* through performance—it's something you *nurture* through presence. When you let go of the need to rehearse, you actually make space to relate. You begin to notice who sees you without the polish—and choose to invest where you're valued, not just needed.

Empowering Tone

You are not required to keep auditioning for acceptance. You don't have to shrink to stay connected. You can show up as your whole self—even in rooms where not everyone will applaud—and remain whole. Because in the right spaces, authenticity isn't a risk; it's a requirement. And when you start living from that truth, your relationships begin to reflect your *reality*, not your disguise.

* * *

Chapter 7 Summary and Closing: Performative Connection

Emotional effort, strategic over-accommodation, and being "easy to work with" might get you noticed—but often not for the right reasons. You've always been the one people rely on. The one who smooths things over, takes the blame, and shows up confident and prepared. But deep down, you've outgrown the version of yourself that longs to be chosen by softening your presence or ignoring your instincts. As one character said in *The Holiday*:

"You, I can tell, are a leading lady. But for some reason, you are behaving like the best friend."

This applies to the men reading this, too—it's time to stop being the supporting cast in your own life. You're not just the problem solver, the dependable one, or the sidekick. You are the main character of your story.

This chapter asked you to consider:

- What parts of yourself feel hidden, even in your most valued relationships?
- What would it mean to stop just performing and begin truly participating?
- Who truly sees you—and who only sees the version that benefits them?

But more than anything, this chapter encourages you to *start becoming*: to lead with honesty instead of tactics, to build relationships that accept your whole self, not just your role, to walk away from applause that demands a mask. You deserve connections that don't feel like auditions.

✨ Chapter 7: Performative Connection – Pause for Perspective

Virtue: Sincerity

Sincerity isn't loud or showy—it's the quiet strength of choosing to live honestly in a world that rewards performance. It's no longer bending yourself into versions that fit someone else's comfort. To show up—not perfectly, but truthfully—is to risk being misunderstood, underestimated, or even dismissed.

But clarity calls you to a higher purpose: being *known*, not just tolerated. Even when no one else recognizes the quiet significance of your choices, integrity allows you to remain true to your principles. It means prioritizing presence over performance, honesty over convenience, and conviction over charm—especially when the cost is unseen by everyone but you. This chapter invites reflection on where you've taken on supporting roles in your own story:

- What am I rehearsing instead of revealing?
- Which roles have I outgrown, and who am I becoming beyond them?
- Where have I sacrificed genuine belonging for acceptance?
- Who remembers and values me without needing my résumé?

Sincerity teaches you how to stop shrinking your voice to protect someone else's comfort. It helps you distinguish adaptability from erasure—and reminds you that sincerity is not a weakness. It's a quiet form of power. Ultimately, your worth won't be measured by how *agreeable* you were, but by how *authentically* you lived.

👉 Next Steps: Workbook Journal Prompts

For a deeper look at how authenticity, approval, and performance-based connection affect your sense of belonging, refer to the Companion Workbook for Chapter 7.

 ## Personal Notes & Insights

Use this page to capture any quotes, ideas, or personal revelations that surfaced while reading. Let it be messy, real, and yours.

_____

_____

_____

_____

_____

_____

_____

_____

_____

_____

_____

_____

_____

_____

_____

_____

TO THE ONE WHO SHOWED ME I WAS ENOUGH

Intimacy begins when urgency fades—and safety comes from within.

You never expected me to always be "on." I didn't need to impress you, prove myself, or hide my struggles to keep you close. You met me where I was—messy, creative, tired, and hopeful. You never made me feel like I was too much or not enough. You gave me room to breathe, to ramble without editing, to cry without apologizing, and to exist without explanation.

And in your presence, I learned a sacred lesson: I don't have to earn love by being useful. I don't have to perform to be embraced. I don't have to hide my fears to be respected. With you, I wasn't a project to fix or a person put in your life to serve you. I was a human being to experience—and to have experiences with. That kind of relationship doesn't just bring comfort. It restores.

Thank you for helping restore my faith and hope in people. Thank you for providing me with a safe place to land. Thank you for showing me that friendships can be the strongest and most intentional connections we can build. Thank you for showing me that intimacy shouldn't be rushed or forced. This is a bond that has developed over time. A bond that will never be broken.

With clarity,
Shante

CHAPTER 8
EMOTIONAL SAFETY AND INTIMACY

Emotional safety isn't created by access but through consistency, care, and discernment.

Chapter 8 is all about the stage that comes after the performance ends, the stage where you will undoubtedly find yourself asking, "Where do I feel safe enough to be the real me?" Because honesty without safety isn't intimacy—it's exposure. Not all connections are secure. We often confuse vulnerability with trust, but in reality, we've been oversharing and overexplaining in spaces that never earned our trust. We've mistaken access for closeness—urgency for depth. But emotional safety demands more. It asks:

- Who keeps my truth with care?
- Who listens without attempting to fix or control me?
- Who sees me beneath the performance?

And even more importantly: **Am I a safe space for myself?** This chapter will help you understand what emotional safety truly feels like, recognize when it's missing, and learn how to start honoring intimacy as something nurtured—not assumed. Because not everyone deserves full access to you—and real intimacy begins with knowing who can be trusted with it.

Defining Emotional Safety and Intimacy

Emotional safety isn't just about avoiding harm; it's about creating spaces where truth can be shared and connection can grow. When you feel emotionally secure:

- You're not bracing for their inevitable withdrawal of affection.
- You don't need to worry that your vulnerability will be turned against you.
- You can show up without having to act or apologize for your feelings.

When emotional safety is missing, your nervous system often knows before your mind catches up. It will show you through chronic pain, headaches, gut tension, numbness, and burnout. It can also impact your sex drive. Those gut feelings you've been taught to ignore? They're signals, not overreactions.

Recognizing Emotional Safety and Emotional Danger

Safety isn't always announced—it's felt. You'll notice it in the silence after you speak, in how your truth is held, or in the shift that happens in your body after the conversation ends. Are you grounded—or gutted? Let's break it down.

☑ When Safety Is Present

- You speak without hesitating, apologizing, or shrinking.
- Silence feels like space, not tension.
- Honesty doesn't damage the relationship.

⊘ When Safety Is Absent

- You rehearse, overshare, or stay silent to "keep the peace."

- You scan the room before you speak, and replay it all afterward.
- You feel unsure instead of supported—like you left more disconnected than when you arrived.

That's where intimacy comes in—not the performative kind, where vulnerability is rushed to secure closeness or avoid rejection. But the kind that builds slowly. The type that nourishes. The kind that respects your nervous system, not just your words.

What Does Intimacy Mean?

Intimacy is emotional closeness founded on consistency, care, and honesty. It isn't established through oversharing or access—it's nurtured through mutual investment and the ongoing presence of safety. Recognizing safety is only the beginning. Once you identify what helps you feel emotionally grounded, the next step is learning what kind of closeness can be built on that foundation. Intimacy says:

- I can be seen and still respected.
- I can be known without being exploited.
- I can stay close without losing myself.

Previously, we introduced the concept of hospitality of the heart: the act of opening your inner world and inviting others into it. This chapter expands on that idea, providing a more in-depth examination of how emotional intimacy is cultivated between individuals. From a gardening perspective, the word "'cultivate"' refers to a labor-intensive process of breaking up and preparing the soil for sowing or planting. It is a necessary process that involves using the right tools and timing to create a healthy environment for plant growth. The same could be said of building intimacy in a relationship. It's not a mad dash to the finish line. The right tools and time are needed to develop true intimacy.

Attempting to fast-track that process often results in weeds permeating our relationships. When your relationship lacks true intimacy, you become emotional strangers to each other. Without emotional closeness, even regular communication can feel empty. Connection without depth leads to performance, not presence. This doesn't mean giving everyone unfiltered access to your inner life. It takes faith, discernment, and wisdom to ask:

- Who is truly safe to trust?
- When is the right time to open up, and what should I share and what should I keep personal?
- Why am I choosing to entrust myself to this person?

Genuine intimacy involves the extent to which you reveal yourself and how safe you feel while doing so. It's not just disclosure; it's discernment. It's not about performance; it's about mutual participation. And it grows best in spaces where closeness isn't rushed or demanded—but invited, slowly and intentionally.

📖 Story: The Unsent Text

She typed out the message three times. The first version was raw—a flood of feelings, frustration, and unmet needs. The second version attempted to soften it, reframe it, and make it easier for him to understand. The third was short and clean, almost sterile. It explained, but didn't express. It protected, but didn't connect. And then she deleted them all.

Not because her feelings weren't real. Not because she stopped wanting to express herself. But because she finally asked herself a question she'd never thought to ask before:

"Will he handle this with care, or just . . . handle it?"

She knew how it would go; he'd read her message, maybe even respond with some mix of logic and defensiveness. But afterward, she'd feel like she always did—overexposed, underseen, and somehow both too much and not enough. That night, she didn't send the text. She wrote in her journal instead. Not that silence was an easier choice, but because clarity had shown her that **not every truth needs to be shared in every space.** Some truths need tending, not telling.

Maturity is knowing the difference. That was the night she realized emotional intimacy wasn't about being brave enough to be vulnerable. She'd done that too many times already. It was about being wise enough to protect what was tender until it could be held with respect. And that's the difference emotional safety teaches you: clarity quiets the urge to prove. But for many of us, that urge doesn't go away easily. It manifests in other forms—such as oversharing or overexplaining—especially when we're still searching for belonging in unsafe spaces.

* * *

Oversharing, Overexplaining, and the Price of Unmerited Access

When emotional safety and intimacy are missing, we often compensate by giving more of ourselves than is required—or wise. We overexplain to gain understanding. We overshare to feel connected. But here's the truth: more information does not create more intimacy. Oversharing and overexplaining are not acts of openness; they are often survival strategies born from emotional scarcity.

We aren't just sharing to connect—we're bracing against rejection. We flood the space with words, hoping that if we give enough, we'll be accepted, validated, or at least not misunderstood. Both habits usually stem from the same unspoken fear: "If I don't give enough, they'll abandon, judge, reject, or forget me." So instead of sharing with intention, we share in excess—trying to control how we're perceived, hoping that quantity will compensate for the absence of safety.

That's how false vulnerability is born. You say too much, give too much, explain too much—not because you lack boundaries, but because you're afraid those boundaries will be misread. You overexpose yourself, hoping that more words will shrink the distance between perception and truth. But safety isn't earned through excess—it's established through mutual investment and emotional consistency.

Clarity teaches us this: you don't have to flood the room to prove you belong in it. Emotional safety isn't purchased with explanation; it's built through discernment and time.

Reframe: How Support Becomes Pressure

Sometimes, the "support" we seek becomes dependency. Ask yourself: *Where in my life am I asking someone to give what I haven't learned to carry myself?* That's not judgment—it's self-awareness. When we rely on others for constant comfort or clarity, we risk losing our own grounding. So what does it mean to ask for **presence**, not **pressure**?

- **Presence** means their attention is with you—without demanding solutions.
- **Pressure** turns them into fixers or saviors. Your emotions become their assignment.

☑ **Example:**

Presence asks: "Can I vent for five minutes? You don't have to fix it—I need to get it out."

Pressure asks: "You're the only one who understands me. I don't know what I'd do if you weren't here."

And what does it mean to ask for **connection** rather than **correction**?

- **Connection** is about being seen, heard, and met—not fixed.
- **Correction** shifts control, outsourcing your discernment and direction.

☑ **Example:**

Connection asks: "I'm struggling and just need someone to sit with me for a moment."

Correction asks: "What should I do? Tell me what I'm doing wrong."

Emotional Accountability Check

Asking for feedback is healthy. Expecting someone else to supply your answers is not. When you hand your growth to others, you outsource your agency.

Recognizing this difference helps you cultivate connections that are both safe and mutual. Because even when someone appears emotionally fluent—able to talk about feelings or show vulnerability—it doesn't mean they're emotionally safe. And that's where understanding the difference between **emotional availability** and **emotional safety** becomes essential.

* * *

Emotional Availability Versus Emotional Safety

Emotional Availability = Capacity to Engage: This is the willingness and ability to connect on an emotional level.

An emotionally available person:

- Shows up consistently and pays attention to emotional cues.
- Can express their own feelings and receive yours without shutting down.
- Offers depth through empathy, honesty, and responsiveness.

Think of it as the door being open. They're emotionally present—but that doesn't always mean it's safe to walk through.

Emotional Safety = Capacity to Protect. This is about how your emotions are handled once they've been shared.

An emotionally safe person:

- Listens without judgment, minimizing, or redirection.
- Respects boundaries and never weaponizes vulnerability.
- Creates an atmosphere where you can show up authentically—without performing, shrinking, or overexplaining.

Emotional safety confirms: *You can bring your whole self here—and you won't be punished, misunderstood, or manipulated for doing so.*

How They Differ

You can have one without the other—and that difference can completely change how you connect.

- **Emotionally available but not safe** → Open and expressive, yet inconsistent or boundary-poor. They may overshare, demand closeness, or mishandle your truth.
- **Emotionally safe but unavailable** → Kind and respectful, but detached. They won't harm you—but they may not truly engage, leaving you unseen.

In short: Emotional availability opens the door. Emotional safety makes it safe to step inside.

Clarity helps you recognize when both are present—because anything less will leave you either *longing for intimacy* or *hurt by it*.

When Both Are Missing

Some people are neither emotionally safe nor available. They deflect, withdraw, or mock vulnerability—leaving you managing their discomfort instead of honoring your own truth.

Without availability, it's one-sided.

Without safety, it's risky.

And without both, it's not just difficult—it's damaging.

Can Someone Be Available but Not Safe?

Absolutely—and this is where confusion often begins. These individuals are expressive and emotionally open, but unpredictable in how they handle depth. They might:

- Overshare or trauma-dump to create quick intimacy.
- Expect vulnerability they haven't earned or reciprocated.
- Use emotional expression as a strategy—to build closeness, control perception, or steer the narrative.

They're open but inconsistent. Vulnerable, yet boundary-poor. Sometimes they ask for your truth not to connect, but to collect—and what they collect, they might later use against you. This isn't intimacy. It's *exposure without protection*.

When Someone Is Both Safe and Available

This is the kind of connection your body recognizes before your mind can name it. You breathe easier. You speak more freely. You stop rehearsing. They offer:

- **Consistency** – Presence that isn't dependent on performance.
- **Attunement** – Awareness of shifts in you, with genuine curiosity.
- **Boundaries** – Invitations without pressure; openness without intrusion.
- **Reciprocity** – Mutual sharing that builds balance, not dependency.

You feel safe—not because they say the right things, but because they listen with care.

Active Listening as a Sign of Safety

Active listening is one of the most evident signs that emotional safety and availability coexist. It's not just hearing—it's honoring.

It looks like:

- Eye contact that reassures, not intimidates.
- Body language that signals engagement, not distraction.
- Silence that feels spacious, not dismissive.
- Questions that show care, not interrogation.
- Reflections like "I hear you," or "That sounds really difficult."

Listening isn't just a skill—it's an act of stewardship. The way someone listens in small moments reveals whether they can be trusted in deeper ones.

* * *

Client Vignette: The Pause That Changed Everything

I once worked with a client, a director renowned for her composure and quick problem-solving skills. Her team respected her competence but kept an invisible wall between themselves and her. During one session, she admitted, "I think I'm a good leader, but people rarely open up to me until something's already broken."

We explored her team's feedback, and a pattern emerged: she was listening to fix, not to feel. Whenever someone shared a struggle, she moved into solution mode within seconds. Her intention was pure—she wanted to help—but her timing made others feel rushed and unseen.

So we practiced something simple: silence. The following week, she had a one-on-one with a team member who'd been disengaged for months. Normally, she would have jumped in with advice. This time, she didn't. She listened—really listened—and allowed the silence between his sentences to breathe.

He finally said, "I thought you were going to tell me what I did wrong."

She smiled and replied, "I just want to understand."

That conversation changed their dynamic. he became more communicative, more confident, and within weeks started contributing ideas again. Later, Renee said, "I didn't realize that my need to help was actually making people feel unheard."

Active listening isn't passive—it's power restrained. It tells people, "Your experience matters more than my response." It proves safety not through words, but through stillness.

* * *

Expectation of Trust and Its Evidence

Entrustment is sacred—but it should never be blind. It's not about trusting someone instantly; it's about watching how they handle access over time. A wise leader knows this well: though people are drawn to them, they don't rely on these people. They never confuse temporary enthusiasm with loyalty. They know that:

- **Flattery** feeds the ego; **honor** respects the soul.
- **Intrigue** is sparked by novelty; **commitment** endures through faithfulness.
- **Attention** shines for a moment; **devotion** withstands time.

Entrustment doesn't confuse access with safety or expression with intimacy. It asks, *Who has demonstrated the character to value what I give as a treasure, not as leverage?*

Words are easy; follow-through is the tangible evidence of trust. Below are four everyday situations where blind trust often appears—and what to look for instead.

💔 Romantic

They said, "I'm not like the others. You can trust me."

You believed the promise—but when accountability arrived, they vanished. Blind trust became heartbreak.

Lesson: Don't rush into vulnerability. Observe how they honor your honesty—and what happens when you're no longer convenient.

🏠 Family

They said, "You can always count on me. We're family."

Yet when you set a boundary or asked for empathy, they dismissed your feelings or made you feel guilty. You trusted the title—*family*—not the treatment.

Lesson: Proximity doesn't equal safety. Being familiar doesn't mean they've earned access to your heart.

🤝 Friendship

They promised, "I'll always be there for you."

But when hardship came, they fell silent—or made your pain about them. You offered grace for old times' sake, but history doesn't guarantee reliability.

Lesson: Just because someone "knew you when" doesn't mean they can handle who you are now. That's not judgment—it's wisdom.

💼 Professional

A manager said, "We see your potential; a promotion is coming."

You gave more, stayed loyal—and watched the opportunity vanish behind polite praise. You trusted potential, not patterns.

Lesson: Don't confuse compliments with commitment. Watch for consistency—credit in meetings, follow-through in feedback, and truth in timing.

Some people mean well but simply don't have the internal steadiness to carry what's sacred. And that's why the next step in discernment isn't about blame; it's about recognizing who has the *capacity* to be trusted—and who was never meant to hold that weight.

* * *

The Breach of Gossip and Misused Trust

Even when someone seems emotionally available, the real test of safety isn't how they listen—it's what they do afterward. Gossip, back-channeling, or casually "sharing your story" isn't harmless chatter. It's a breach of stewardship. When your private words become someone else's talking point, it reveals they were more interested in information than intimacy. Gossip exposes three truths about a person:

- **Character** – Do they value integrity over influence?
- **Capacity** – Can they hold sensitive truths without leaking them?
- **Consistency** – Do they show the same respect in your absence as in your presence?

When someone repeats what was entrusted to them—whether to bond, brag, or fill silence—it's evidence of immaturity. No matter how warm or attentive they seemed in the moment, gossip unmasks a lack of emotional safety. Here's the rule that rarely fails: If they gossip *with* you, they will gossip *about* you.

That's why intimacy requires more than openness—it requires **discretion**. A safe person doesn't parade your story; they protect it. They understand the difference between *sharing a connection* and *distributing content*.

Gossip Isn't Always the Villain

Not all gossip is malicious. Humans naturally talk about one another—it's how communities bond and share life. The key is *intention and impact.*

- **Neutral Gossip**: "Jane is engaged," "John got the promotion," "Lisa bought a house."
  - This kind of talk builds connection and a sense of belonging. It's social glue, not poison.

- **Relational Gossip**: "Did you hear about the changes she made on the project?"
  - This type manages reputation and expectation—it shapes workplace culture and trust.

- **Betrayal Gossip**: "Did you hear that Jane is thinking about leaving John?"
  - This type repeats something personal that was shared in confidence. It crosses the line. It erodes intimacy, proving the person may be *available to hear* but *unsafe to hold.*

The first strengthens the community. The second influences perception. The third corrodes connection. The distinction isn't in the conversation itself—it's in **the care behind it.**

Client Vignette: When Work Friendship Meets Gossip

I once coached a client—I'll call her *Alex*—who struggled with blurred lines between professional and personal relationships at work. She had grown close with a colleague—I'll call him *Jordan*. They weren't just coworkers—they had lunch together, shared personal updates, and spent time outside of work. That closeness made Alex feel safe leaning on Jordan when work became stressful. Jordan seemed emotionally available—always asking how she was doing, always ready to listen. One afternoon, Alex confided in him about a conflict with their manager, trusting their friendship both in and out of the office.

A week later, things shifted. The manager's tone grew distant, her demeanor more critical. Alex soon discovered why: parts of her private vent had resurfaced through the office grapevine. Jordan had repeated her words—not maliciously, but under the guise of "sharing concern." He'd told others, "I'm just worried about Alex; she seemed really upset about how the manager handled things."

On the surface, it sounded caring. In reality, her private emotions had been repackaged as office talk. What began as **relational gossip**—the kind that shapes perception—had turned into **betrayal gossip**. Jordan had been emotionally available—he asked, he listened—but he wasn't emotionally safe. Because what Alex entrusted wasn't protected; it was redistributed.

* * *

Coaching Insight: When "Sharing Concern" Crosses into Betrayal

Jordan likely believed he was being helpful by "voicing concern" so the manager could be more understanding. But here's the crucial difference:

- **Responsible concern** asks, "Alex, would you like me to mention this to the manager, or do you prefer to handle it yourself?" It respects consent before carrying someone else's truth forward.
- **Betrayal gossip** skips that step. It recasts what was shared privately for a new audience—often softened with language like, "I'm just worried," or "I thought you should know."

Regardless of tone, the result is the same: exposure disguised as empathy. When emotional availability isn't paired with emotional safety, people feel heard in the moment—but harmed in the aftermath. Discernment bridges that gap.

Reader Self-Check: Navigating Safety in Sharing

1. How to Tell if Someone Is Safe to Confide In

Before handing over your truth, look for *evidence*, not promises:

- Do they keep confidence, or "slip" details under the pretext of concern?
- Do they listen without rushing to solve or redirect?
- Do they show reliability in small things as well as big ones?

If these aren't consistent, your truth may not be safe in their care.

2. How to Recognize When "Concern" Is Actually Gossip

Sometimes gossip dresses up as care. The language often sounds like:

- "I just thought you should know . . . "
- "I'm worried about them, so I mentioned it . . . "
- "I didn't mean any harm; I was only sharing concern."

Genuine concern seeks consent first. If they didn't ask before repeating your words, it wasn't concern—it was exposure.

3. How to Practice Safe Availability Yourself

Being emotionally available doesn't make you emotionally safe. To embody both:

- **Regulate before responding.** If you're overwhelmed, say, "I want to give this my full attention. Can we circle back?"
- **Hold confidence carefully.** Unless given permission, what's shared with you stays with you.
- **Offer presence, not pressure.** You don't have to fix their pain—you only need to honor it.

Even when someone has good intentions, another truth remains: **intention isn't the same as capacity.** Emotional safety doesn't just require kindness—it requires readiness. This is where discernment helps you honor both your needs and their limits.

* * *

Capacity Is a Type of Discernment

Sometimes a person isn't indifferent—they're just at their limit. That doesn't make them unsafe; it makes them *unready*. They may lack the emotional, mental, or even physical capacity to hold what you're sharing.

Discernment recognizes this without resentment. It doesn't punish people for what they can't give. It protects *you*—allowing you to withhold what cannot yet be honored, without guilt or self-doubt. And it dignifies *them* by acknowledging their limits without condemnation.

Respecting Boundaries and Guarding What's Sacred

When you're emotionally drained and desperate to feel seen, it's easy to ignore red flags and confide in someone who isn't ready to receive you. But choosing not to share isn't always a matter of fear—it can be a matter of clarity. It's not rejection; it's recognition.

When you hand over the most tender parts of yourself to someone who hasn't shown the ability to protect them, you risk more than rejection. You risk emotional harm. Often, the damage isn't done out of malice—it's done out of *immaturity*, or lack of awareness. Some people don't know the weight of what they've been given.

That's why emotional regulation matters. When your emotions surge, the urge to "vent" can masquerade as relief—but unfiltered venting, especially without consent or boundaries, often becomes trauma-dumping. Emotional maturity is the pause between impulse and disclosure. It allows you to assess the safety of the space before you speak and to share from a place of *stability* rather than urgency.

Your emotions, your experiences, your healing—these are treasures, not transactions. Discernment helps you protect both yourself and others without apology. Let wisdom guide *what* you offer, *when* you offer it, and *to whom*. Because emotional safety isn't just about who's willing to listen—it's about who will **guard** what you entrust to them.

It's easy to mistake familiarity for safety. But safety isn't about the moment; it's about the *pattern*.

- Some leaders promise growth but never create space for it.
- Some people care but are inconsistent in that care.
- Some love you deeply—but still don't listen.
- Some are present—but not protective.

You can care about someone's heart and still not give them yours.

Trustworthiness Check

Before entrusting something sacred, pause and ask yourself:

- **Consistency** – Do their actions match their words? Trust isn't proven through promises—it's patterned over time.

- **Care** – Do they treat your vulnerability with reverence, not as leverage? A trustworthy person protects your truth, instead of profiting from it.
- **Capacity** – Do they have the space and self-awareness to receive what you're sharing? Readiness matters as much as intention.

If even one of these is missing, intimacy becomes a risk rather than a refuge. But when all three are present, **entrustment becomes wisdom in motion.**

* * *

🌙 Emotional Arc – Chapter 8: Emotional Safety and Intimacy

Core Tension

You were taught to believe that honesty automatically creates closeness. But honesty without safety isn't intimacy—it's misplaced trust. Too often, you've shared deeply in spaces that weren't ready to hold your vulnerability. Instead of being met with care, you were met with inconsistency, dismissal, or exploitation. The result wasn't connection—it was guardedness.

Positive Balance

Clarity reveals that intimacy doesn't require full access—it requires mutual respect. When you build safety first, your relationships begin to take on a different quality. You honor yourself by discerning what to share and when, and you honor others by recognizing their capacity and limits. Expectations become healthier. Conversations feel lighter because you're no longer performing for belonging. Silence no longer feels awkward—it feels like peace.

You begin to notice who can sit with you through the pause, who checks in because they were paying attention, and who protects what you share as something sacred. These are the connections that restore you. They become spaces where you can exhale, be understood, and still feel safe.

Empowering Tone

You are not required to trust everyone who reaches out to you. You have permission to wait, observe, and choose where you invest your heart. The right people won't just *receive* your openness—they will *protect* it. When you practice discernment, intimacy transforms from something you chase into something you *cultivate*. And through that cultivation, you realize that your presence is not merely valuable—it's sacred.

* * *

Chapter 8 Summary and Closing: Emotional Safety and Intimacy

When it comes to emotional intimacy, safety is the fertile soil—and clarity is the water that sustains growth. Without both, even a well-meaning connection can leave you uprooted. Chapter 8 revealed the layers between presence and protection, between being heard and being held. It clarified that emotional safety isn't just about closeness—it's about how consistently someone can honor your truth without reshaping it for their comfort.

It also exposed how behaviors like overexplaining and oversharing often mask fear—not because you lack a desire to connect, but because you've learned to protect yourself by proving yourself. You've tried to stay safe by staying understood. Yet proper safety doesn't come from volume—it comes from discernment. Here's what emotional safety looks and sounds like in real life:

- Safety is someone who listens to understand—not to fix, defend, or redirect.
- Safety sounds like "Take your time," "I hear you," or silence that doesn't feel like punishment.
- Safety is the freedom to share without scanning for judgment or withdrawal.
- Safety is consistency over time, not intensity in moments.

Intimacy isn't a sprint; it's a slow, steady walk. It's not about sharing everything quickly—it's about sharing intentionally, based on observed trust. Clarity helps you stop offering your truth as a peace offering. It enables you to discern who's truly ready, not just curious; who's capable, not just available.

That doesn't mean you're closed off—it means you're wise. This isn't about withholding; it's about pacing connection in alignment with self-trust. You're not hoarding your love; you're stewarding it. You're not suspicious—you're faithful to your own safety.

So when you catch yourself overexplaining, oversharing, or overextending, pause and ask:

- Is this expression—or is this emotional auditioning?
- Has this connection nurtured the version of me I'm becoming—or kept me performing as the version I outgrew?

Because you can value someone—and still choose to protect the parts of yourself that are healing and the parts that have finally learned peace.

✦ Chapter 8: Emotional Safety and Intimacy – Pause for Perspective

Virtue: Faith as Discernment

Faith goes beyond belief—it's trust expressed in motion. It's not passive hope or naive optimism. It's a conscious choice to honor your truth even when the outcome is unclear. Not because you know how it will be received, but because you finally know your truth deserves to exist—shared at the right time, with the right people.

There's an ancient proverb that says: *Don't cast your pearls before swine.* This isn't a warning against generosity—it's wisdom about discernment. It's a reminder that not every treasure is meant to be handed over to every person. When something sacred is placed in careless hands, it often gets trampled—not out of malice, but because the receiver doesn't know its worth. And sometimes, the damage isn't just to what was shared—it's to the heart that shared it.

Put plainly: you can't give all of yourself to everyone. People who do not value your emotional, spiritual, or personal treasures may misuse them, whether intentionally or unknowingly. Faith teaches you not to fear this—but to filter through it. Faith doesn't rush revelation. It invites timing. It reminds you that intimacy isn't proven through exposure—it's cultivated through trust.

Faith says, "I will be honest, but I will also be careful," and "I don't audition for love—I recognize where it already feels safe to land."

Let faith anchor your pace. Let discernment guide your openness. And let clarity show you who has the character to meet you with both. Clarity has a way of creating distance before it builds peace. When you start protecting your truth, you notice who steps back—and who steps closer. Some relationships quietly dissolve under the weight of your boundaries, not because you stopped caring, but because you stopped overextending.

It's in that quiet space—after you stop explaining, fixing, and reaching—that the loneliness sets in. You begin to realize that healing doesn't always come with company. But this solitude isn't punishment; it's preparation. It's the sacred in-between where you learn to feel safe inside your own presence again.

The next chapter explores that space—the tender isolation that follows clarity, and the strength that's found when connection must begin within.

☞ Next Steps: Workbook Journal Prompts

For deeper reflection on how emotional safety, intimacy, and entrustment shape your connection with others, turn to the Companion Workbook for Chapter 8.

 # Personal Notes & Insights

Use this page to capture any quotes, ideas, or personal revelations that surfaced while reading. Let it be messy, real, and yours.

_____

_____

_____

_____

_____

_____

_____

_____

_____

_____

_____

_____

_____

_____

SECTION THREE
ISOLATING RECONNECTION

*The distance isn't rejection—
it's reconnection, with you.*

TO THE ONE I COULDN'T TAKE WITH ME

I had to leave you so I could get closer to me.

You showed me some loyalty—but not the kind I wish to imitate. You demonstrated a connection, but solely on your conditions. I gave freely, poured out my energy without hesitation, and stayed longer than was sensible. For a time, I believed I was loving. But clarity revealed the truth: it was service without stewardship.

My longing to be needed clouded my judgment. What I believed was principled devotion was actually misguided loyalty—a connection driven by guilt, history, and obligation. Not mutual appreciation and respect. I became skilled at over-functioning and silencing my voice. But I was never the subject matter expert on myself. I can admit now: it wasn't healthy love. And yet, my love for you remains, a testament to the depth of our connection.

It's become clear that, contrary to Mary J. Blige's assertion, love without limits can often lead to self-abandonment and neglect. I've come to realize that I can no longer offer a version of myself that erases me. Letting go wasn't easy, but holding on would've meant betraying the woman I am becoming. I'm releasing the version of us that only survived by my compliance. I'm taking with me those shared moments of laughter and support, even though they were inconsistent. I'm leaving behind the guilt, the imbalance, and the weight of holding together what was never mine to carry alone. And with that release,

I'm finally finding myself, and I'm choosing to prioritize self-love, self-respect, and dignity.

With clarity,
Shante

CHAPTER 9
ISOLATING RECONNECTION

When clarity costs connection but fosters alignment.

Every chapter thus far has focused on internal work—untangling motives, confronting betrayals, setting boundaries, and breaking patterns that fueled burnout. Each breakthrough has been an inward shift, often accompanied by anger, guilt, hurt, and grief. But this chapter marks a turning point. Isolating Reconnection is when clarity begins to emerge outwardly. It's the moment your inner self shifts to influence your external choices.

It's when distance becomes necessary—not because you stop caring, but because you can no longer afford to betray yourself in the name of connection. This stage is challenging. It may feel confusing, painful, and lonely, but it is also deeply freeing. Every step back helps you see yourself more clearly. Taking pauses from the chaos creates space for clarity to grow because **you can't hear your own voice until you silence theirs.**

🗣 Client Story: The Mother

I had a client who was an overachiever and came into coaching because she was tired of pursuing goals "that had no value" to her.

We ended up discussing her relationship with her mother, and she shared the following:

"Every win I share feels like a competition. Every struggle I confide to her becomes a lecture. Somehow, even my pain comes back to her."

The cycle for her was unrelenting: joys were minimized, hurts were dismissed, and a "no" was recast as betrayal. Nothing felt safe enough for her to bring home. The breaking point occurred after a phone call in which her mother called her "selfish" for choosing distance to reflect and think about the state of their relationship. Her mother hung up on her. My client, for the first time, refused to call her back. Months went by. Keeping that distance wasn't impetuous; it was intentional. Her silence wasn't punishment toward her mother; it was her way of protecting herself. She still loves her, but she has stopped sacrificing herself to keep a bond that has emptied her. She told me recently:

"At times, I mourn her as if she's dead. Because in a way, that version of our relationship is. I had to bury it to keep myself alive."

Sometimes the grieving begins long before the goodbye—and that grief is what ushers in a new kind of reconnection: the one that starts with you.

* * *

What Is Isolating Reconnection?

You don't notice the silence at first. It's gradual—the kind that creeps in after you stop reaching for people who no longer reach back. One by one, the voices that used to fill your days grow faint, not because of conflict, but because of clarity. It's strange how peace can sound so much like loneliness at first. You've released the relationships that relied on your overfunctioning, the ones that required you to shrink to stay connected. But now that the noise is gone, you're left with the sound of your own breathing—and the question that follows: *Who am I when no one is mirroring me back?*

This chapter explores the emotional dissonance of healing—how clarity can make you feel both stronger and more isolated. It's about what happens in the fragile space that follows awareness, when clarity compels you to start releasing relationships that no longer align with your peace. It's the space where solitude can feel like solitary confinement—but also where your peace begins to breathe again.

My client's story captures the essence of Isolating Reconnection: the outward expression of inward clarity. It begins when you stop betraying yourself for the sake of a relationship and start creating space from those who repeatedly distort, dismiss, or drain you. It's not about cutting people off in anger or bitterness. It's about refusing to keep feeding relationships that cannot—or will not—honor your humanity.

Isolation here isn't abandonment; it's realignment. It's clear evidence that your breakthroughs are not just internal insights but also external choices. In the stillness of distance, reconnection begins—not with the person who refuses to meet you, but with yourself and the truth you no longer rationalize or argue away.

The Stages of Isolating Reconnection (Cyclical, Not Linear)

Isolating Reconnection isn't a single decision. It's a process—one that rarely moves in straight lines. Some days you'll feel clear and steady; other days, grief or guilt will creep in and make you second-guess your choices. These emotional waves are part of the journey, not proof of failure. Each stage carries both shadow and light—the ache of release and the gifts that rise in its place.

Denial

At first, denial whispers that maybe it wasn't that bad—that you overreacted, that the good moments outweigh the harm. Denial shows up as bargaining, minimizing, or rewriting history to soften the truth. It feels protective because if you can convince yourself that nothing was really wrong, you don't have to face the loss.

- **Shadow:** Avoiding truth delays healing.
- **Light:** When denial breaks, clarity settles in. You start to see the whole picture instead of fragments. This clarity validates that your pain was real, your boundaries mattered, and your choice to create distance wasn't imagined or impulsive.
- **Ask Yourself:** What truth am I trying to soften so I don't have to face it?

Practice: Write down the exact moment of clarity when you realized distance was necessary. Keep it close as a reminder when doubt creeps back in.

Anger

Anger rises—at how long you tolerated mistreatment, at yourself for not seeing it sooner, at how your loyalty was taken for granted. This stage burns hot but clarifies what deserves your protection.

- **Shadow:** If left unchecked, anger can turn inward into self-blame or outward into bitterness and revenge fantasies that drain you.
- **Light:** When acknowledged, anger sharpens awareness. It reveals where your boundaries were crossed and fuels self-respect and courage to stand firm in your "no."
- **Ask Yourself:** What boundary is this anger pointing me toward?

Practice: Write one clear sentence naming what you will no longer accept. Repeat it when anger resurfaces.

Grief

Grief mourns not only what you lost, but also what you hoped for and never received. It comes in waves—heavy or quiet, but always honest.

- **Shadow:** Grief can feel endless, pulling you into exhaustion or tempting you to return to stop the ache.
- **Light:** Grief honors your capacity to love and long for better. It reminds you that your desire for mutual, safe connection was never wrong—and that desire can guide you toward healthier relationships ahead.
- **Ask Yourself:** Am I grieving the person as they were, or the version I imagined them to be?

Practice: Give grief a container. Set a timer for 15 minutes to journal, cry, or sit with it fully, then gently re-engage with your day.

Guilt

Guilt says: "I owe them," "I'm selfish," "I should explain one more time." But most guilt at this stage is an echo of old rules you no longer live by.

- **Shadow:** Guilt can pull you back into over-explaining, apologizing, or over-functioning to ease discomfort.
- **Light:** When examined, guilt becomes a teacher. It reminds you that loyalty without respect isn't love—and protecting yourself isn't betrayal; it's integrity.
- **Ask Yourself:** Whose voice is this guilt speaking in—mine or theirs?

Practice: When guilt rises, make a two-column list: guilt's demands versus what honoring yourself looks like instead. Notice how differently each voice feels in your body.

Sadness

Sadness is the quiet ache of absence—missing their presence, the history, the belonging, even the comfort of routine.

- **Shadow:** Sadness can blur truth, making you mistake longing for love.
- **Light:** Sadness softens you, making room for gratitude—for the good that did exist and for new connections that won't cost your peace.
- **Ask Yourself:** What do I miss—the person, or the comfort of not being alone?

Practice: Create a playlist that begins with songs that allow you to sit with your sadness, then gradually shifts to lighter ones that move you forward.

Loneliness

The quiet feels heavier than the chaos once did. You may long to return, not because it was safe, but because it was familiar.

- **Shadow:** Loneliness convinces you that no one will understand, tempting you to settle for unsafe closeness.
- **Light:** Loneliness creates room for hope and curiosity. It opens the door to connections with people who value who you are, not what you provide.
- **Ask Yourself:** Am I longing for them, or for relief from the emptiness?

Practice: Schedule intentional time with someone safe—a friend, mentor, or group where you can be your authentic self.

Emptiness / Boredom

When you're no longer consumed by their moods or demands, the *unoccupied time* can feel restless and ungrounded. This is often the hardest stage because it asks: *Who am I without them?*

- **Shadow:** Emptiness can mimic identity loss, as if without them, you are no one.
- **Light:** Emptiness is freedom in disguise. It opens the space to rediscover your voice, your interests, your talents—the parts of you buried beneath survival.
- **Ask Yourself:** What's one small interest or hobby I've ignored that I want to explore in this new space?

Practice: Choose one activity this week that belongs only to you—read, walk, draw, cook, sing, or sit in your own company.

Because these stages aren't linear—you'll cycle through them more than once. When the wave comes, name it, ask the question, and return to practice. Yet even after you've named the waves, another tension may surface—the tug between what you know and what you were taught to tolerate.

* * *

Cognitive Dissonance: When Awareness Conflicts with Conditioning

Cognitive dissonance is the mental tug-of-war between clarity and conditioning—the truth you now see and the old beliefs that still try to hold you. This *double-mindedness* creates instability. It makes you want to do the very things you no longer wish to do. Even when you understand the truth, parts of you may still resist because they were trained to equate peace with compliance.

🗣 Client Vignette – Cognitive Dissonance

One of my clients described this as feeling "split in two." After distancing herself from her father, she felt relief; for the first time, she could breathe without the weight of his criticism. A week later, guilt crept in—*What kind of daughter doesn't call her dad?* The quiet felt unnatural, even wrong. So she called him back. Within minutes, the cycle returned—the dismissal, the twisting of her words. She hung up and cried, realizing she had just abandoned herself again.

This is the heart of cognitive dissonance. It often pulls people back into harmful patterns because the tension feels unbearable. Learning to sit in that tension—without rushing to fix it—is part of developing emotional regulation. The back-and-forth doesn't mean you're weak; it means your conditioning hasn't yet caught up with your clarity.

- **Head:** "This person is harmful. I can't keep living like this."
- **Heart:** "But I still love them."
- **History:** "I've always been the one who stayed. What does it say about me if I stop now?"

A Path Forward

- **Name It:** When the push-pull appears, tell yourself, "This is dissonance, not truth."
- **Ground It:** Write down the moment that gave you clarity—the argument, the betrayal, the dismissal. When doubt creeps in, reread it.
- **Reframe It:** Instead of asking, "Am I making a mistake?" ask, "What part of me is struggling to catch up to my clarity?"

Reflection Question

When I feel drawn back into old patterns, is it because I genuinely want the relationship—or because I'm seeking relief from the discomfort of dissonance? That's where the shift begins. Because when you stop reaching for instant relief, you can finally face who's been waiting all along: you.

* * *

The Question of Identity: Who Am I Without Them?

The hardest part of creating distance isn't just missing the person—it's realizing how much of your identity was shaped around them. For years, you might have been the peacekeeper, the strong one, the responsible one, the caretaker, the achiever. Those roles gave you purpose and belonging, even when they came at the expense of your own needs.

When you finally step back, it's natural to feel disoriented. This is where clarity redirects your focus inward with a deeper question: *Who am I without their expectations defining me?* You may discover that parts of yourself were built for survival. Some traits can be released. Some can be reshaped. Others are worth carrying forward—this time with intention.

💬 Client Example

One client told me she had always been the "fixer." The youngest of four children, she became a caretaker early. Her mother passed away, leaving her father to raise them alone. Two siblings battled alcohol addiction; another often left her children for others to care for while she pursued her personal life. To protect their father from the chaos, everyone covered for everyone else.

My client, trying to hold the family together, became the parent to them all—even to her dad. If there was a conflict or a crisis, she rushed to smooth it over. If someone was struggling, she offered help before they asked for it. Over time, that role became her identity. Burnout eventually exposed the truth: her "fixing" wasn't love—it was fear. Fear of being excluded. Fear of losing control. Fear of becoming irrelevant in a family that thrived on dysfunction. Her worth came from being useful, not from being herself.

With clarity, she began to make different choices. She realized her compassion wasn't the problem—her control was. So she reframed her role as something healthier: offering support freely, not out of guilt or obligation. She went from "fixer" to "compassionate sibling and daughter."

She still has moments when she feels the urge to step back into control, but she recognizes it now as a signal—not a calling. The survival trait hasn't disappeared; it's been transformed into something that promotes her growth and encourages accountability within her family.

Reflection Prompt

Think of one trait you recognize in yourself that was developed through survival.

- What healthy version of it could I grow into?
- Why does growing in this way matter to me?

Even after you start to redefine who you are without them, the habits that once kept you safe will still try to pull you back. Awareness brings strength, but it also brings vulnerability. And that's where the real work begins—learning to steady yourself when old patterns come knocking.

* * *

The Mirror Moment

After years of making decisions based on his needs, moods, and limitations, I finally ended the relationship. And when the noise stopped, I looked in the mirror—and didn't recognize the woman staring back at me. I wasn't the old Shante, the one who existed before him. She was gone—and truthfully, I didn't want her back. That version of me, in her brokenness, had chosen him. But I also wasn't the Shante I became to survive him—the one made of sharp edges, built to protect and defend myself emotionally and psychologically.

Eventually, those edges gave way to silence. Not because I was weak. Not because I didn't know how to break his spirit right back. And not because he had succeeded in breaking me. I chose silence because I didn't want to become him. I had refused to let him break my integrity. And honestly, I also chose silence because I was exhausted. For the sake of my sanity, I decided not to keep punching immovable walls.

That day, as I looked at myself in the mirror, all I could feel was pity for the reflection staring back—a woman who'd been in survival mode for so long she'd forgotten what stillness felt like. I wanted to succumb to mourning the loss. Understandably, I had been in that state for weeks after he left.

And then it hit me—*girl, why?* You've been called to peace.

And maybe this sounds dramatic, but I thought of the movie *Waiting to Exhale*. I had no business watching that movie at fifteen, but even then, I understood grown folks' pain—at least intellectually. But I didn't *feel* it until decades later, standing in my own bathroom, realizing I no longer had to hold my breath.

So I looked at myself in the mirror again. And instead of focusing on the sadness in my eyes, I slowly let a small smile form. I inhaled deeply, then exhaled. In that moment, I realized the quiet in my home—the same quiet that once felt like punishment—was no longer disconnection. It was freedom.

That's what *Isolating Reconnection* does when you allow it to do its work. It removes what once drained you so you can finally hear your own voice again—deeply, freely, and without reservations.

Of course, peace isn't the end of the story. The moment you exhale, life will hand you new tests—moments that ask, "Will you hold your boundary this time?" Peace doesn't erase patterns overnight; it simply gives you the strength to face them differently. So when the pull of old habits returns—and it will—that's when practical anchors can steady you.

* * *

Practical Anchors When You Slip

Clarity doesn't mean perfection. You might step away for a week only to find yourself explaining, apologizing, or reaching out again. That doesn't erase your progress; it simply reminds you that healing isn't a straight line.

One of the most discouraging aspects of Isolating Reconnection is the belief that setbacks mean failure. But a slip isn't a collapse—it's an invitation to practice coming home to yourself again. Growth isn't measured by how perfectly you hold the boundary; it's measured by how gently and how quickly you recover after wavering. Because healing is practice, not performance, clarity needs structure—something to hold onto when your emotions start to drift. That's where the 'three Rs come in." Here's a tool to help you realign whenever you feel yourself slipping.

The Three R's for Managing Setbacks

When you notice yourself slipping, please don't rush to fix it. Slow down and listen instead. Every setback is a signal—a reminder that something in you still wants comfort, understanding, or stability. Rather than judging the impulse, trace it back to its source. Because healing is practice, not performance, clarity needs structure—something to hold onto when your emotions start to drift. That's where the three R's come in."

Recognize—Observe what's happening without judgment. Naming the truth weakens shame's hold.

- **Tell yourself:** *"I'm calling because I feel lonely, not because this relationship suddenly became safe."*

Reflect—Reflection separates new priorities from old patterns. Often, what feels like missing the person is really missing the role you played in their life.

- **Ask yourself:** *What am I truly needing right now—comfort, connection, validation, or clarity?*

Redirect—Choose a safe way to meet that need without compromising your integrity.

- **Comfort** → Wrap yourself in a blanket, take a bath, journal, pray, or listen to a grounding song.
- **Connection** → Text a trusted friend, join a group that connects you to your interests, or spend time with someone who truly sees you.
- **Clarity** → Reread your journal entries, clarity statements, or affirmations of who you're becoming—and remember why you chose distance in the first place.

💡 A Gentle Reminder

Setbacks don't mean failure; they tell you you're still practicing. Every realignment builds trust in yourself and strengthens the resilience you'll need for what's ahead. Once you've learned how to return to yourself, the next lesson is learning how to stay soft without surrendering your boundaries.

Compassion is not a pass for harm; it's a posture of understanding. It lets you say, "I see why you are the way you are," without saying, "I'll keep letting it cost me." You can hold both—empathy for their story and accountability for your boundaries. Distance doesn't make you cold—it makes you clear. This is what healing and growth look like in real time: clarity that steadies, compassion that softens, and boundaries that hold.

* * *

🌙 Emotional Arc – Chapter 9: Isolating Reconnection

Core Tension:

This stage feels confusing because clarity pulls you in one direction while conditioning pulls you in another. You know this person drains you, yet part of you still longs for the comfort of their presence. The silence feels heavier than the chaos, and even as you reclaim your space, you still ache for what was familiar.

Positive Balance:

Clarity reveals that the distance you've created is not punishment—it's protection. It is not abandonment—it's alignment. The emotions that surface—denial, anger, grief, guilt, sadness, loneliness, emptiness—aren't signs of failure; they're signs of awakening. They prove you're finally allowing yourself to feel what performance and proximity once forced you to suppress.

Empowering Tone:

The discomfort of this season doesn't mean you've made the wrong choice—it means you've made a different one. Every time you resist falling back into old patterns, you strengthen your self-respect and self-esteem (See Chapter 4). At first, the silence feels unbearable—every unreturned call, every quiet evening, every empty seat reminds you of what used to be. But over time, the same silence that once felt suffocating begins to open up. It becomes space to hear your own thoughts, to rediscover what brings you joy, and to remember who you are without someone else's voice directing your worth.

And what about the distance? Initially, it feels like a wound that will never heal; as if something precious has been torn away. But when you resist the urge to throw a Band-Aid on the wound by circling back, that distance transforms you. It becomes a process of healing. It reveals where they end and where you begin. It gives your heart the space to stop functioning in survival mode and start preparing to flourish.

You don't have to rush the process or fill the void. Just let the distance do its work.

* * *

Chapter 9 Summary and Closing: Isolating Reconnection

Isolating Reconnection isn't about turning away from others—it's about turning toward yourself. It's proof that you'll no longer trade dignity for counterfeit closeness. While this stage may stir discomfort, it also makes space for relief, clarity, empowerment, and hope.

Each stumble may feel like failure, but every return to yourself is a victory. Relief comes when you realize you no longer have to brace for the next storm. Gratitude rises as you honor both the love you gave and the courage it took to walk away. Lightness follows as you set down what was never yours to carry.

And in the quiet left behind, something new begins to emerge—something that doesn't wait for circumstances to change. It steadies your emotions, quiets your thoughts, and reminds you that you can breathe freely without asking permission. That's not avoidance. That's peace of mind. This process won't always feel triumphant. Some days will be unsteady, even disorienting. But it serves a purpose—preparing you for the next milestone: **The Space In Between**, that tender, unsteady ground between who you were and who you're becoming.

✦ Chapter 9: Isolating Reconnection – Pause for Perspective

Virtue: Peace

Some of you might roll your eyes at this, but I've been honest this far—no point stopping now. Peace at this stage isn't performed calmness. It's not the glossy, commercial kind where people twirl through grocery aisles or dance down city streets, pretending life just "clicked." (And if it were, remember the long list of side effects that come at the end of the commercial.)

Peace is also not the Instagram version—walking the beach in slow motion, sipping lattes reflectively in cafés, or posting passive-aggressive quote after quote about "letting negative people go" as if pain evaporated overnight. You might nod in agreement now, but be honest—how many times have you scrolled, compared, and measured your healing and growth by someone else's highlight reel?

The peace we're talking about doesn't photograph well. It transcends human logic, planning, and performance. It doesn't need a filter because it isn't meant to impress anyone. It runs deeper—guarding your entire inner world. It steadies the heart by calming emotions, reshaping desires, and purifying motives. It steadies the mind by quieting the noise, easing confusion, and restoring perspective.

This isn't peace that comes from circumstances getting better. It's peace that emerges despite circumstances—peace that keeps you steady when nothing else can. The type that doesn't need an audience or a like button.

☞ Next Steps: Workbook Journal Prompts

For deeper reflection on the emotions, setbacks, and identity questions that surface in this stage of Isolating Reconnection, turn to the Companion Workbook for Chapter 9.

 ## Personal Notes & Insights

Use this page to capture any quotes, ideas, or personal revelations that surfaced while reading. Let it be messy, real, and yours.

TO THE ONE WHO ALWAYS NEEDED A PLAN

Clarity came. Now what?

Modesty. Faith. Hope. That's what you're learning to embody now because clarity revealed the truth: your obsession with always having a plan was never about excellence—it was about survival. Don't depend on others, and you won't be let down. Don't leave space for the unknown, and you won't be abandoned. You are filled with laughter as you reflect on how poorly you tried to control your own path—convinced that certainty was safety, when in reality, anxiety was the one guiding you.

You held too tightly to the destination, missing the beauty of the journey. Now, with clarity, you no longer walk in a state of urgency. You've let go of the illusion of complete control and have chosen to embrace a more sacred pace.

You move forward not by your own blueprint, but with trust, patience, and awareness. Your steps are grounded in humility and strengthened by self-worth. You've learned that the path takes shape with each step you take. And the pinnacle? It isn't just a destination—it's the journey itself.

With clarity,
Shante

CHAPTER 10
THE SPACE IN BETWEEN

It may seem like nothing is happening, but everything is taking root.

Chapter 9 taught you that distance isn't rejection—it's a return to yourself. But once that distance is established, another challenge begins: learning how to live within it. This is *the space in between*—the awkward, uncertain, often frustrating middle ground where you no longer fit the patterns of your past but aren't yet steady in your future. It feels like a holding place, where clarity exists but hasn't yet been proven. It's not the first step—that was courage. It's not the finish line—that's still unfolding. This is where endurance takes shape—where you keep walking without applause, validation, or a clear map.

The temptation here isn't just to return to what's familiar; it's to mistake stillness for stagnation. Yet this space is not punishment—it's preparation. The proving ground where patience is tested, conviction is built, and quiet hope begins to take root. This chapter is about learning to wait intentionally—to stay steady when nothing feels certain—and to trust that even here, in the in-between, something within you is quietly taking root.

The Space in Between: When the Middle Creates a Sense of Emptiness

I first learned about this season at nineteen, when Iyanla Vanzant referred to it as *"In the Meantime."* Back then, I didn't fully understand it—or maybe I didn't yet have the patience or wisdom to live it. More than twenty-five years later, I recognize how real it is—and how much resilience it takes to honor this stage without rushing through it.

The in-between often triggers self-doubt. It feels like leaving one life but not yet settling into the next. Looking back shows you can't return; looking forward feels like staring into fog. There are no milestones, no applause, no visible proof of progress. The pause can seem like idleness, stirring doubts about whether your efforts are moving you forward. But this isn't emptiness—it's incubation.

This phase doesn't just test your patience—it tests your conviction. Waiting feels passive only when you forget its purpose. Remember: stillness isn't punishment. Growth is happening beneath the surface. And when you've been conditioned to chaos, this quiet can feel like boredom—but don't mistake peace for emptiness. Keep holding your ground, keeping promises to yourself, and staying aligned in ways you never have before. This is the soil where your next self takes root—and where true transformation begins.

🗣 Maya's Story (Personal / Relationship)

When my client, Maya, initially separated from her toxic partner, she expected freedom to feel like relief. Instead, it felt like a loss. The quiet was deafening. She had known silence before—the kind that came from living separate lives under one roof—but this silence was different. It was unfamiliar, unsettling, and honest. Every corner of her apartment echoed with reminders of what once was.

The emptiness grew so loud she reached for anything familiar. She scrolled through old text threads, reconnected with people she'd outgrown, and even let her friends talk her into hollow dates—attempts to "get over him" that only left her emptier. She realized it wasn't his love she missed—it was the predictability of a wound she already understood.

She confessed to me, "It's not that I want him back—it's just that I don't know what to do with myself now." Her clarity was intact, but the pain of standing still made retreat seem easier than waiting. In her quietest moments, she could still hear her grandmother's voice: "Better the devil you know than the devil you don't."

* * *

The Discomfort of Waiting

The void doesn't stay silent for long. Emptiness quickly mirrors every doubt and fear you thought you'd outgrown. The middle doesn't just feel quiet—it feels unbearable. Nights stretch longer. The clock ticks louder. You scroll endlessly, hoping distraction will dull the ache. Some days you pace with nervous energy; other days you sink into stillness that feels like cement. This is what the in-between does: it shakes loose every anxious thought you once buried beneath busyness.

It's not just time you're struggling with—it's identity. You're no longer who you were, but you're not yet confident in who you're becoming. That uncertainty feels like exposure. Titles, roles, routines—the things that once anchored you—have vanished. Without them, you feel naked. How do you introduce a version of you that's still unfolding? This is the tug-of-war between patience and panic. Waiting doesn't just test your ability to stay still; it tests your conviction to stay true when nothing feels certain. And here's the truth: many of us would rather return to what's been harming us than trust what's forming. We call it comfort, but it's really control—managing the discomfort of waiting strips that illusion away.

Here's the reframe: **if it didn't feel awkward, it wouldn't be a transformation.** Discomfort isn't proof you're failing—it's evidence that you're shedding what no longer fits. This is where emotional regulation becomes your lifeline. It's not about suppressing emotion—it's about staying present with it. Sometimes that means resisting the urge to text an ex just because you're lonely. Other times, it's taking a breath instead of reacting out of fear. These small acts of restraint build endurance. They teach you how to sit *in* the meantime without collapsing *into* it.

🗣 Jordan's Story (Career / Professional)

Jordan finally quit the job that had worn him down for years. The relief was instant—until the in-between hit. Mornings felt strange without a routine. He scrolled job boards for hours, then stared at rejection emails as if they were proof he'd made a mistake. "Maybe I should just ask for my old job back," he thought. "At least I knew who I was there."

The truth was, Jordan didn't miss the work—he missed the structure, certainty, and validation that came with the title. Without it, he felt exposed, restless, and impatient for the next chapter to begin. The ache of the in-between made him crave the false security of his old role—the familiar chains he once called stability—rather than trust the freedom ahead.

* * *

The Hidden Work Underneath the Surface

The hardest part of the in-between is that it looks unproductive. Nothing feels solid; it's easy to assume nothing is happening. But beneath the surface, movement begins. Think of a seed underground. For weeks, there's no sprout—just undisturbed soil. Yet in that unseen space, roots are forming, and a seedling is preparing to break through. The same is true for you. Progress here rarely looks like breakthroughs; it shows up in subtle shifts you almost miss:

- Saying no without drowning in guilt.
- Recovering from disappointment in days instead of weeks.
- Choosing silence over the text you'll regret.

These are your unseen roots—quiet choices that no one else sees but that make you unshakable. Maya didn't realize it yet, but every time she resisted the urge to look back, she was freeing space for what was next. Jordan couldn't see it either, but every rejection he faced without retreating strengthened his conviction.

Who Am I Becoming?

The most fragile question in this stage is identity. You've shed the clothes that no longer fit, but haven't yet found the ones that do. That limbo is unsettling. The temptation is to rush into new roles or keep pretending, but both are subtle forms of self-betrayal. But here is something empowering: **You don't have to define yourself right now—you only have to *notice*.**

For some, this is about uncovering what's always been true. For others, it's rebuilding from the ground up, trying on new ways of being. Either way, clarity calls for honesty. Each act of exploration—each moment you stay curious instead of critical—builds confidence in who you're becoming.

Practical Reflections: The "What's Me?" Questions

This season invites you to identify, not idealize. Use these questions as mirrors to see what's shifting within you:

- *What feels natural to me, even when no one's watching?*

- *What feels heavy, forced, or like a mask I've been wearing?*
- *Which habits or traits are part of my design—and which are defenses I created to survive?*
- *Where am I being more honest now than I was before?*

Identity work isn't about arriving at a perfect answer; it's about uncovering the real one. Perhaps that means choosing a hobby to enjoy without trying to monetize it. Maybe it's answering, "I don't know yet," when someone asks about your next move. As you rediscover who you are, find something stable to anchor you—a practice, a value, or a ritual that keeps you from drifting back into old identities when uncertainty pulls at you.

The longer you stay in the in-between, the more you begin to notice: healing isn't loud. It's subtle, rhythmic, and often uneventful. But that's the point. Stillness teaches you to live without constant proof of progress. It invites you to become patient—with purpose.

* * *

Patient with Purpose: Enjoy Your Own Company

🗣 Maya's Middle Phase (Personal / Relationship)

Some nights, the calm still felt suffocating. Maya would catch herself scrolling through her phone, hovering over her ex's name—or the names of people she'd already outgrown. But more and more, she stopped herself. Instead of sending a message, she began journaling her thoughts. Instead of numbing herself with endless scrolling, she started cooking meals she genuinely enjoyed. And instead of replaying where things went wrong, she began focusing on the qualities she could build on to meet her future with strength.

It didn't erase the pain, but it brought her comfort—and a sense of connection. Each time she chose to sit with herself instead of filling the silence, she strengthened a different kind of muscle: the ability to be at home in her own company.

- Spend time with yourself in ways that nourish, not numb.
- Cook a meal, light a candle, wear your favorite outfit—for you.
- Take a walk without hurrying. Create something without posting it.

Let ordinary moments become sacred ones.

🗣 Jordan's Middle Phase (Career / Professional)

Some mornings, Jordan woke with regret heavy on his chest. Former colleagues would message him about new changes at the company—promotions, reorganizations, raises. Each update stirred the question, "Did I make a mistake?" The rejection emails that followed only added to the doubt.

So he started small. He built a daily routine that gave his days structure. He reflected on his values before applying for new roles, learned new skills online, and wrote down what he truly wanted next. The doubts still showed up, but they didn't stay as long. What once spiraled for weeks now settled in days. Each quick recovery was proof of quiet progress—of resilience being built from the inside out.

Jordan's and Maya's growth may have looked different, but their lessons are the same: **solitude isn't punishment.** It's practice—an invitation to rediscover your voice and the rhythm of your own becoming.

Reclaim Your Voice

In the in-between, silence can feel like losing yourself—but it's actually the space where your authentic voice begins to return. You don't have to force it; you just have to use it. Even a whisper counts.

Anchors That Ground You

Write five "I" statements to reorient yourself:

- I value . . .
- I choose . . .
- I believe . . .
- I no longer . . .
- I am . . .

Each declaration helps you reconnect with conviction—the quiet kind that doesn't need validation.

Ground Yourself in the Present

When anxiety pulls you into *what-ifs*, redirect to *what is*:

- Five things you can see
- Four sounds you can hear
- Three things you can feel
- Two things you can smell
- One thing you can taste

It's not about perfection—it's about presence.

Reframe the Waiting

Your mind may label this phase *failure, complacency,* or *punishment.* Counter it:

- Instead of "I'm stuck," say "I'm becoming."
- Instead of "Nothing is happening," say "The work is happening beneath the surface."
- Instead of "I don't know who I am anymore," say "I'm discovering who I want to be."

A Self-Compassion Pause

When anxiety peaks, ask yourself: "What would I say to a friend in this exact moment?"

Then offer yourself that same grace. These small acts of gentleness keep you from abandoning yourself while you wait.

* * *

The Gift of Quiet

You don't have to fill the silence to prove you're okay. At first, quiet feels like an enemy—reminding you of what you've lost, what you don't yet have, and how far you still think you need to go. But, throughout history, people have sought solitude not to escape but to *listen*. Solitude has never been idleness—it's always been training. Your quiet seasons work the same way: not wasted space, but shaping space. This stage carries its own hidden gifts:

- **Anticipation** → hope for what's ahead, even when its shape is unclear.

- **Relief** → the peace of no longer betraying yourself just to belong.
- **Trust** → the discipline to let your roots deepen before your branches stretch.

Every time you stay in the moment, you strengthen your foundation. Every time you choose alignment over urgency, you invest in the version of yourself that can withstand what's next. Eventually, that silence stops echoing your doubts and begins reflecting your growth. It becomes a teacher—revealing peace in places you once overlooked. What once felt unbearable softens into opportunity: to breathe, to notice, to create, to find a rhythm that belongs only to you.

Quiet doesn't erase uncertainty, but it reframes it. Instead of asking, "When will this be over?" you begin to ask, "What is this teaching me now?" That shift is its own kind of clarity—sometimes soothing, sometimes exposing, but always sacred. The in-between holds both relief and restlessness in the same breath. In many ways, it echoes what you learned about gratitude and resentment: proof that clarity often comes wrapped in paradox.

When the Space Is Interrupted

Not everyone stays long enough in the in-between to grow from it. Many try to fast-forward through discomfort by filling the silence with substitutes for peace. When the quiet feels unbearable, we reach for noise—something to numb, distract, or reassure us that we're still moving.

It looks different for everyone: another drink, another scroll, another hookup, another purchase, another "I'm fine." For some, it's numbing with alcohol or drugs; for others, it's hiding in work, the gym, food, service, or even spirituality—anything that feels productive enough to disguise avoidance.

- The danger isn't necessarily in the activity itself but in the intention behind it.
- If what you reach for is meant to **distract you**, it delays your healing.
- If what you reach for is meant to **develop you**, it deepens your transformation.

The space in between isn't meant to be filled—it's meant to be *faced*. It's where you learn to choose what heals you over what hides you. Waiting becomes sacred when you stop sedating your growth and start strengthening it.

Both Maya and Jordan reached that crossroads—the point where distraction could've been easier than development. What they chose instead reshaped how they saw themselves.

🗣 Maya's Closing Vignette

Maya sometimes still missed what she left behind—but she no longer let the ache decide for her. What once felt like unbearable silence became open space: a place to breathe, notice her own needs, and rediscover the parts of herself she'd buried in old relationships. She still had lonely nights, but she also woke to mornings where pride quietly replaced regret. Progress didn't arrive in grand gestures—it showed up in ordinary choices. Each moment of self-respect rebuilt her confidence. She learned that peace didn't have to be earned, joy didn't have to be loud, and strength often whispers before it roars.

🗣 Jordan's Closing Vignette

Jordan didn't land his dream job overnight, but he no longer measured his worth by a title. The simple routines he built—reflecting, learning, volunteering—gave him stability that success had never offered. Rejections still hurt, but they no longer defined him. He began to see the in-between not as failure, but as a foundation. Each day he showed up for himself, he grew steadier, wiser, and more assured. For the first time in years, he wasn't just performing success—he was living in alignment with it.

This tension doesn't just manifest in romantic and professional losses. It plays out in every kind of separation—whether it's family, friendship, career, or community. The instinct to run from discomfort is universal. But each time you resist numbing and choose awareness instead, you become someone who can hold peace even in the unknown.

* * *

Emotional Arc – Chapter 10: The Space In Between

Core Tension

The in-between is both *relief* and *restlessness*. Relief because you've stopped betraying yourself. Restlessness because you haven't yet grown into the life you're building. One moment, you're proud you walked away; the next, you wonder if you made a mistake. That contradiction wears on you, making you question whether the change was worth it.

Positive Balance

Clarity reminds you that peace often comes disguised as a pause. The absence of chaos feels foreign at first, but it's not failure—it's transition. Each moment of uncertainty is your new life stretching its legs, learning to hold steady before it runs. Growth isn't the absence of doubt; it's the decision to keep going despite it.

Empowerment

Strength here isn't about finishing—it's about refusing to abandon yourself while waiting. It's choosing not to send the text you'll regret, not to take the job that betrays your values, not to collapse back into old roles to feel grounded. Awkwardness is proof of growth. Power multiplies when you stop asking, "When will I arrive?" and start asking, "How can I stay aligned right now?"

* * *

Chapter 10 Summary and Closing: The Space in Between

This stage will stretch your patience, rattle your confidence, and tempt you to retreat. But the in-between does not have to be wasted—it's the workshop where conviction is built in small, hidden choices. Your task here isn't to rush clarity but to remain steady within it. Practice the unseen decisions: honoring your truth, resisting quick relief, and staying present in uncertainty. These aren't minor acts—they are the roots of change.

Adopt this mindset: *I may not yet be who I'm becoming, but I will not betray myself now.* Progress here is loyalty—to yourself, to your clarity, and to the future you are preparing. And when the waiting feels unbearable, remember: this pause is laying stone beneath your feet, demanding a strength that shortcuts can't deliver. What you choose here determines how ready you'll be for what's next.

✨ Chapter 10: The Space in Between – Pause for Perspective

Virtue: Patience

Patience is often mistaken for doing nothing, but here it becomes strength in motion—the steady refusal to collapse under pressure, which could cost your clarity. This kind of patience doesn't just wait; it *endures*. It makes you stronger in the very places that once made you quit.

Though awkward at times, patience opens the door to joy—the quiet pride of showing up for yourself even when there is no witness to it. Waiting with intention isn't complacency, laziness, nor the naivety and tolerance of harm. It's patience with purpose. Every pause, every moment you resist looking back and start leaping forward, is proof that you are becoming someone who can carry clarity with confidence. That's where patience meets joy—when you realize your life isn't on hold. Even in the waiting, you are building strength for what's coming.

When the waiting refines your patience, forgiveness refines your heart. What happens next isn't about holding still—it's about releasing what still holds you.

Personal Notes & Insights

Use this page to capture any quotes, ideas, or personal revelations that surfaced while reading. Let it be messy, real, and yours.

_____

_____

_____

_____

_____

_____

_____

_____

_____

_____

_____

_____

_____

_____

☞ Next Steps: Workbook Journal Prompts

For deeper reflection, turn to the Companion Workbook for Chapter 10. Use the prompts to explore the anchors that steady you, the temptations that test you, and how patience can become strength rather than struggle.

TO THE ONE WHO STOPPED WAITING

Forgiveness starts with yourself.

It was difficult to admit—but for a long time, you held onto the hurt because you were waiting for an apology. Not just for closure —but for validation. You relied on that apology to affirm your worth. To recognize your effort. To honor all that you gave of yourself. Because if they could say, "I see you . . . I'm sorry," it would mean that your presence mattered, and your love was appreciated. Your pain wasn't invisible.

But with clarity, you learned something deeper: Just because someone can't recognize your value doesn't make you worthless. A diamond found in the dirt is still a diamond. The dirt doesn't define it—only covers it. And if someone picks it up, can't see past the dust, and throws it back down, that doesn't make it any less precious. It just means they didn't know what they were holding.

You stopped waiting for the apology. You stopped tying your healing to someone else's recognition. You stopped asking for repair from the same hands that caused the damage. And that choice? That was the moment you stepped out of survival and into refinement. You will keep shining. Not because they finally saw your light . . . But because, through faith, you chose never to let it be extinguished again.

With clarity,
Shante

CHAPTER 11
DISCERNING FORGIVENESS

Forgiveness isn't permission. It's release—with discernment.

In Chapter 10, you learned to steady yourself in the space between clarity and becoming. But as you begin to move forward, you may discover a heavier kind of weight—not the uncertainty of who you're becoming, but the emotional residue of what (or who) hurt you. You may not be looking back, but the burden remains—old wounds, unmet apologies, and unspoken betrayals. You've created distance. You've done the work to separate physically from what no longer serves you. But now, clarity presents a new question:

What will it take to let go—mentally, emotionally, and spiritually—so you're no longer dragging the weight of pain into places meant for peace?

🌱 A Note Before We Begin

This might be the most controversial chapter—the one that challenges you the most. Not because it's the hardest to read, but because it might be the most difficult to apply. People interpret forgiveness in many different ways, and some of those definitions are deeply personal, cultural, or spiritual. Depending on your beliefs, background, and wounds, the word itself might trigger resistance.

Let me clarify this: this chapter isn't about obligation. It's not about being the "bigger person." It's definitely not about pretending you weren't hurt. My goal isn't to provide you with the definition of forgiveness, but to invite you to consider a more empowered version of it. I'm here to offer a new perspective—one that helps you recognize what truly happened, let go of what no longer serves you, and move forward without carrying the same burden.

You don't have to agree with everything written here. You don't even need to be ready to apply it right now. But I invite you to stay open—not to me, but to yourself, and to the possibility that forgiveness might look different than what you were taught.

* * *

Why This Matters

You've allowed yourself to pause—to reset, to grieve, to begin again. You've let silence reintroduce you to your own voice. You've drawn boundaries, pulled back from what no longer fits, and taken ownership of your story. But now, the next threshold emerges:

What do I do with all the pain I've carried this far?

Clarity doesn't just create distance from who you used to be—it brings you face-to-face with the emotional baggage it left behind. The grief. The resentment. The betrayal. The loneliness that lingers after you've walked away. These emotions don't vanish once you find your voice. In fact, they often get louder—because the noise of dysfunction has faded, and in its place is a clear, quiet truth: that you've been hoodwinked and bamboozled.

That's where forgiveness steps in. Not as a performance. Not as erasure. But as a **disciplined act of mercy** toward yourself.

How Do You Define Forgiveness?

Before we begin, ask yourself: *What do I picture when I hear the word forgiveness?*

Definition	What it means
Letting Go	Releasing anger, resentment, or the need for revenge.
Excusing	Saying "it's okay" or "I accept it," even if it wasn't.
Reconciliation	Repairing the relationship and returning to closeness.
Moral Duty	Something I must do to be a good person.
Forgetting	Pretending like it never happened.
Internal Reset	Choosing peace, even without repair.
Other	I define it as: _____

All of these are real interpretations. That's what makes forgiveness so confusing—religion, culture, trauma, and personal values have all shaped how we see it. But confusion doesn't mean you're broken. It means your **discernment** is waking up.

Common Forgiveness Myths We've Been Told

Let's confront some of the most common lies we've been told about forgiveness:

Myth	Truth
Forgiveness = Forgetting	No. Healing doesn't require amnesia.
Forgiveness = Reconciliation	No. Reunion is optional, not automatic.
Forgiveness = Excusing	No. Excusing real harm is self-betrayal.
Forgiveness = Weakness	No. Releasing pain is strength.
Forgiveness = Obligation	No. It's a choice, not a punishment.

Myth	Truth
Forgiveness = Instant	No. It's often a process—and not a linear one.

These myths create pressure. They rush you. They ignore nuance. And they turn something deeply personal into a performance. The truth is, forgiveness isn't a single, clean act or a neat process—it exists on a spectrum and adjusts depending on the context and the relationship.

* * *

Forgiveness on a Spectrum

Forgiveness isn't one-size-fits-all. It lives on a spectrum—because not all harm is equal, and not all healing looks the same. From small slights to serious violations, each point on the spectrum asks for a different response. Your approach to forgiveness will naturally shift depending on the *depth of the wound* and the *nature of the relationship*.

Spectrum Overview:

- ◐ Minor Annoyances →
- ◔ Patterns of Disregard →
- ● Serious / Chronic Abuse

◐ Minor Annoyances Spectrum

These are the everyday bumps: sharp tones, missed texts, and minor misunderstandings. Forgiveness here is about grace—letting go so resentment doesn't pile up over time. This is where "forgive and forget" actually works. You acknowledge the mistake, offer compassion, and move on.

This kind of forgiveness keeps relationships healthy and emotionally breathable. It's not about being passive—it's about choosing peace over pettiness.

◉ Patterns of Disregard Spectrum

As we move along the spectrum, forgiveness takes on a different meaning. This is the middle of the spectrum—where harm is no longer occasional but *repetitive*. The friend who dismisses your boundaries. The colleague who takes advantage. The partner who erodes your dignity over time. Forgiveness here isn't just about "forget it and move on." It requires **discernment**:

- Open dialogue
- Setting clear boundaries
- Emotional distance if needed
- Re-evaluating whether the relationship is still safe and aligned

Here, forgiveness may mean letting go internally while making profound external changes.

◉ Serious / Chronic Abuse Spectrum

This is the far end: trauma, betrayal, manipulation, or repeated emotional, physical, or sexual harm. These are *violations* that break trust and threaten safety, not minor annoyances. Forgiveness here—if it happens—is *never* owed. Specifically, when the person isn't asking for your forgiveness, it's never required to occur face-to-face.

Reconciliation is not always the end goal. Protection is.

Forgiveness at this level is not about excusing the past but releasing its power to control your future. It often requires:

- Deep healing work
- External support
- Time, distance, and safety

Sometimes choosing *not* to forgive is an important part of protecting those you love and your dignity.

Sidebar: The Truth About "Forgive and Forget"

Forgive and forget most applies to the first category—minor missteps. Here, forgetting means: I'm not keeping score. I'm choosing not to turn this into a tally sheet. But beyond that? Forgetting becomes dangerous.

- In **patterns of disregard**, forgetting invites repeat harm.
- In **chronic abuse**, forgetting becomes destructive and erases your reality.
- And in both, forgetting is *not* forgiveness—it's *denial*.

True forgiveness, especially in the face of deep harm, says: *I remember. And I will protect my peace. I will not carry this weight forever—but I will not pretend it never happened.*

Memory isn't the enemy of forgiveness—it's the boundary that keeps your peace and dignity. Don't mistake erasing the past for releasing its influence. This is why forgiveness is often misunderstood: a truth meant for minor daily offenses—"forgive and forget"—is all too frequently applied to the entire spectrum.

* * *

Reflection: Where Am I on the Spectrum?

Think about a current or past relationship that still stirs something in you. Where would it fall?

- ◐ **Minor friction** → Small slips that require grace and clarity
- ◐ **Recurring disregard** → Ongoing harm that requires boundaries
- ● **Deep harm** → Lasting wounds that call for protection and distance

What would forgiveness look like in this situation? What do I need to feel safe for forgiveness to happen?

Now ask:

- What would forgiveness *actually* look like here?
- What would I need to feel safe enough even to consider it?
- Is forgiveness even part of what I want—or is what I really need *healing*?

* * *

The Reciprocity of Forgiveness

Forgiveness isn't just something we extend to others—it's something we also *need* ourselves. It's easy to focus on who hurt us, but we've all played the other role: forgetting, disappointing, reacting poorly. No one moves through relationships without needing grace.

Every day, forgiveness lives in small exchanges:

- A friend forgives your lateness.
- A partner forgives your sharp tone.
- A coworker forgives your mistake.

These aren't betrayals—they're human flaws. And without a mutual willingness to both give and receive forgiveness, those flaws accumulate and give rise to resentment.

When Reciprocity Is Absent

When trust is already fragile, even minor missteps get magnified. A forgotten text reads like rejection. A sharp word sounds like contempt. Instead of forgiving the moment, people assign motives—and connection erodes under suspicion.

Why This Matters

This isn't about excusing real harm. Reciprocity is the grace that keeps love, friendship, and even work relationships from fracturing under everyday imperfection. When you forgive small things, you protect the bond. When someone forgives *you*, it reminds you that you're not reduced to your worst moment. This two-way grace fosters resilience and keeps relationships alive despite unavoidable failures.

Reflection Prompt

- Where have I received forgiveness for the small things?
- Where can I extend that same daily grace to others?
- How does remembering my own need for forgiveness shape how I treat others?

But not every wound is a small scratch easily smoothed over by daily grace. Some scars cut deeper—so deep, they don't just test your patience; they stretch the very definition of what forgiveness means. These are the betrayals, the neglect, the violations of trust that shift forgiveness from a mutual exchange into a personal reckoning. This is where forgiveness stops being about reciprocity—and becomes about resilience.

When forgiveness stretches beyond daily grace into profound betrayal, we need more than patience—we need perspective. And sometimes, the stories we were told as children offer more wisdom than we realized.

* * *

✦ Cinderella Wasn't Weak – She Was Wise

What if one of the most familiar fairytales was actually a masterclass in forgiveness?

Cinderella is often dismissed as passive—waiting for rescue, too timid to speak. But maybe we've misunderstood her. She had every reason to grow bitter: she lost her parents early, was betrayed by her family, and was reduced to a servant in her own home. She was silenced, demeaned, and only seen when someone needed something.

And yet, she didn't let cruelty harden her. She remained soft yet discerning, present yet principled. She never begged for love from those unwilling to give it. She preserved her dignity and refused to become like those who hurt her.

Maybe she wasn't a pushover, but a survivor. Just a teenager, she had no therapist, no trauma-informed guide—just resilience, a few unlikely allies, and clarity. She embodied strength without becoming hard, and she offered forgiveness without betraying herself. Her quiet power showed up in how she moved:

- She didn't demand apologies—because she knew she never deserved the harm.
- She didn't explain her worth—she just carried it.

- She didn't seek revenge—she let envy collapse under its own weight.

When the opportunity came, she didn't chase it out of desperation—she received it with readiness. What it took some of us decades to learn, she lived out as a teenager: *Forgiveness is not about reunion—it's about release.*

What Cinderella Teaches Us About Forgiveness

Her story reminds us that forgiveness takes many forms. But one of the most challenging questions we face is this: *Does forgiveness mean reconciliation?* That's where discernment comes in. Letting go of pain is one thing. Deciding if the relationship should be restored is something else entirely.

Reflection Prompt

- Where in my life am I holding out for fairness or apology before letting go?
- What would choosing peace look like for me right now?

* * *

Forgiveness Versus Reconciliation

Cinderella's story shows us that forgiveness doesn't require revenge—but it also doesn't require reunion. You can release the weight of harm without stepping back into a relationship with the person who caused it.

Forgiveness is personal—an inward release that doesn't depend on the other person.

Reconciliation is a relational process—it requires trust, change, and a shared responsibility.

One is about your *healing*. The other is about *restoring a connection*. Confusing the two is how many end up stuck in cycles of harm.

Discernment Compass for Reconciliation

When considering reconciliation, ask:

- **Safety First** → Would reconnection endanger me or others?
- **Patterns Over Apologies** → Has change been proven through actions?
- **Capacity & Willingness** → Does this person *want* to change—and *can* they?
- **Respect Demonstrated** → Are my boundaries honored, or still tested?
- **Shared Responsibility** → Am I the only one doing the repair work?

Reconciliation as a Spectrum

- **No Contact:** Full distance to ensure safety and healing.
- **Limited Contact:** Minimal interaction, on clear terms.
- **Functional Contact:** Connection through necessary roles (e.g., co-parenting, caregiving).
- **Partial Connection:** You accept what they *can* give (logistics, support), but protect yourself from what they *can't* (emotional maturity, accountability).
- **Complete Reconciliation:** Trust has been restored, and both parties have demonstrated consistent change and mutual effort.

* * *

🗣 Client Story: The Father

I once coached a client who was struggling with uncertainty in many areas of her life—but one of the most painful was her relationship with her father. They hadn't spoken much in months. For years, he had dismissed her emotional needs and minimized her pain. She found herself standing at the crossroads of clarity: learning to accept that her father would likely never become the version of him she wished for. Through our work, she came to understand that forgiveness didn't mean pretending he'd changed—it meant releasing the expectation that he ever would.

She began to see the ways he *did* show up: financial help, practical support, and presence during family moments. Reconciliation for her wasn't about blind reunion; it was about gratitude for what he *could* offer, and peace with what he could not. She chose **partial connection**, not denial—and through that acceptance, she found freedom.

When Forgiveness Threatens Others

Forgiveness is personal, but **reconciliation is never private** when others' safety is at stake. If reconnecting gives someone who's harmed a child—or any vulnerable person—continued access, that decision crosses a moral and ethical line. You can forgive in your heart if you choose. But never confuse reconciliation with mercy when it endangers others. Protecting the vulnerable is not vengeance—it's integrity.

Reconciliation is not owed, nor is it proof that forgiveness has occurred. It's a *choice* that lives on a spectrum—one that demands safety, evidence, and radical acceptance of what the other person can and cannot give. Still, not all harm carries the same weight. Some fractures are daily and repairable; others—like betrayal, abandonment, or infidelity—test the very limits of the heart. This is where forgiveness becomes more complex, and **discernment becomes essential.**

* * *

Forgiveness in Betrayal & Infidelity

If reconciliation exists on a spectrum, **betrayal and infidelity push it to its edge.** These are not "minor annoyances," miscommunications, or accidental oversights. They are deep fractures—**breaches of trust that shake self-worth, security, and identity.** This level of betrayal also reveals where we've betrayed ourselves—ignoring red flags, silencing intuition, and over-functioning to keep love alive. This is where forgiveness gets complicated. Some will argue that it's necessary, and to heal, you need to forgive and reconcile. The truth is, depending on the situation, **forgiveness is a personal matter. Reconciliation is situational. And self-respect is non-negotiable.**

Forgiveness as a Choice

As explored in Chapter 4, self-betrayal and relational betrayal are often intertwined. One opens the wound; the other delays the healing. Self-betrayal is when you override your own truth, silence your needs, ignore red flags, or diminish your instincts to preserve a relationship, avoid conflict, or maintain a false sense of harmony.

- It's saying "yes" when you mean "no."
- It's staying silent to keep the peace when your soul is screaming.
- It's putting someone else's comfort above your own well-being.

This is often the **first wound**—the moment you abandon yourself to maintain connection. But when the person you bent for, covered for, or sacrificed yourself for eventually betrays you—through infidelity, manipulation, neglect, or harm—their betrayal doesn't just hurt. It **reopens** the wound you gave yourself.

Because the external betrayal is so glaring, so loud, and so jarring, your focus stays on *them*. Their actions. Their choices. Their damage. And so your own self-betrayal—the original tear in your integrity—**remains in the shadows**. That means healing is delayed. Why? Because the *root* of the pattern—your abandonment of self—is never addressed. You may walk away from *them*, but never return fully to yourself. If you only focus on what they did, you risk bypassing the insight that could stop the cycle.

But if you honor both truths—that they harmed you, and you ignored yourself—then your healing becomes more complete. You grieve what was done. You reclaim what you abandoned. You forgive (if and when you choose). And more importantly, you *restore trust in yourself*. Forgiveness can't be rushed, forced, or demanded. Even if forgiveness happens, reconciliation isn't automatic. Sometimes forgiveness means releasing bitterness while still walking away. Sometimes it means finding peace while keeping the door closed.

If reconciliation is even an option after betrayal, **it must be earned—not assumed**. Apologies are not enough. Healing requires:

- **Consistent actions over time**, not quick fixes or grand gestures.
- **Full accountability**—no minimizing, no blame-shifting.
- **Transparency and humility**, especially around new boundaries.

Without these, reconciliation is not love—it's **betrayal, repeated.**

Reflection Prompt:

- Do I *want* to forgive—or do I feel pressured to?
- If I forgive, can I truly let it go—or will resentment return?
- If reconciliation is on the table, what proof must I see?
- Where do I need to choose **self-respect** over repair?

Betrayal and infidelity remind us: Forgiveness is not weakness. And withholding it is not bitterness. It's discernment—the courage to protect your peace and your future. Because forgiveness without change is cheap. And reconciliation without proof is dangerous.

* * *

Forgiveness as Refinement

Charles Caleb Colton, an 18th-century English writer, once said, "Pure truth, like pure gold, has been deemed unsuitable for circulation because people have found it more convenient to adulterate the truth than to improve themselves."

For those seeking forgiveness, this diluted version is appealing because it avoids accountability. If forgiveness means excusing or forgetting, they never have to face the weight of what they've broken. But grieving is necessary. Without grief, forgiveness becomes entitlement for the offender and repression for the wounded.

- Those who forgive too quickly avoid mourning what they've lost.
- Those who seek forgiveness too quickly avoid mourning what they've damaged.

This isn't freedom—it's a trap. It leaves the offender unaccountable and keeps the wounded person stuck in victim mode. Until grief is faced, forgiveness will continually be cheapened into something it was never meant to be.

Think of silver in a furnace. The flames don't create value—they reveal it. Fire exposes what cannot stay, stripping away denial and illusion. Forgiveness works the same way. Clarity is fire. It forces you to confront betrayal, broken trust, and even your own self-betrayal. Fire alone destroys. But forgiveness refines. Refinement doesn't erase the wound—it defines what survives the fire:

- Let go of bitterness, but keep the boundary.
- Let go of self-punishment, but keep the wisdom.
- Let go of illusions, but keep the truth.

The value was always there—the fire revealed it.

Vignette: The Pottery Studio

She stood in the quiet pottery studio, holding the bowl that had cracked in the kiln. It had looked fine when she shaped it—balanced and beautiful. But something inside wasn't strong enough. Maybe the clay was too thin in one spot. Perhaps the firing temperature revealed a hidden flaw. The instructor walked over and said something she wouldn't forget:

"The fire doesn't cause the crack. It reveals where the structure was already weak."

That bowl couldn't be repaired—not fully. But it taught her something more important: she wasn't bad at pottery. She was learning. And the crack wasn't shameful—it was *information*. Next time, she'd adjust. She'd strengthen what she couldn't see before.

Forgiveness, she realized later, was the same. It didn't mean pretending the bowl wasn't broken. It didn't mean trying to glue it back together to say she had something "whole." It meant using the lesson to make something stronger next time. She didn't need to carry the cracked bowl forever. But she did need to hold what it taught her.

* * *

When Forgiveness Isn't Genuine

There's a danger that lies in **faking forgiveness**—saying the words but not living the truth of them.

- One partner cheats in retaliation.
- The betrayal becomes leverage, used to shame, manipulate, or control.
- Resentment festers beneath silence, eroding the relationship from within.

This isn't forgiveness, it's performance. And performance eventually poisons. Betrayal and infidelity remind us: forgiveness is not weakness, and withholding forgiveness is not bitterness. It's discernment—the courage to choose what protects your dignity and future. Because forgiveness without change is cheap, and reconciliation without proof is dangerous. To heal fully, you can't just release others. You have to face yourself. That's where the real fire begins.

The Process of Self-Forgiveness Through the Fire of Clarity

So far, we've explored forgiving others for their betrayals, limits, and mistakes. But what about the harm you've caused yourself? Sometimes, self-forgiveness isn't about excusing every choice you made. It's about distinguishing regret from condemnation.

- **Regret says:** "I wish I had chosen differently."

- **Condemnation says:** "I am unworthy because of what I chose."

This brings us back to Chapter 4 and the theme of **self-betrayal**—the quiet ache of staying in places that dishonored your truth. Those choices can leave wounds just as deep as the ones others inflict. Forgiving yourself doesn't mean pretending it didn't matter. It means refusing to keep punishing yourself for the clarity you didn't yet have—or weren't ready to trust. It means deciding to stop weaponizing your past against yourself.

How to Recognize the Need for Self-Forgiveness

You may be stuck in self-blame if you find yourself:

- Replaying the same mistake on a loop.
- Silencing your voice because you no longer trust your judgment.
- Believing past choices define your worth.
- Feeling ashamed for staying too long in draining spaces.
- Carrying guilt for ignoring red flags.
- Thinking you somehow *deserve* mistreatment.
- Dwelling on the past so much that it steals your present peace.

Self-Forgiveness in Practice

- **Name It.** Write down exactly how you feel you've let yourself down. Be honest, even if it hurts.
- **Separate Who from What.** What you did is not who you are. Actions can be corrected without defining your identity.
- **Release the Debt.** Ask: "What debt am I still trying to collect from myself?" Then choose to let it go. You owe yourself peace, not punishment.

- **Learn Forward.** Self-forgiveness doesn't erase the past—it equips you to make wiser choices in the future.

Reflection Prompts

- What do I hold against myself that I'd easily forgive in someone I love?
- If I believed I truly deserved grace, how would I treat myself today?
- What's one action I can take that proves I've learned—not that I've failed?

Clarity exposes the wound—but it cannot heal it. Without self-forgiveness, clarity leaves you in the flames—burned, but unchanged. Forgiveness is what lets the fire refine you, not consume you.

* * *

Vignette: The Apology I Owed Myself

She kept replaying the moment in her mind—not the betrayal someone else caused, but the one she committed against herself. It wasn't dramatic. No public spectacle, no slammed doors. Just a quiet choice made behind closed lips:

- She stayed silent when everything in her screamed to speak.
- She accepted the bare minimum because she didn't know if she deserved more.
- She bent herself small one too many times until she forgot her original shape.

And when the truth finally burned its way to the surface, her first instinct wasn't compassion; it was condemnation. How could I have let that happen? Why didn't I leave sooner? What kind of woman keeps showing up for people who keep showing her she doesn't matter? The shame was louder than the facts. And clarity—brutal in its honesty—made it hard to hide. But that same fire started showing her something else:

- That regret wasn't weakness. It was evidence of growth.
- That guilt, if held gently, could become a compass—not a cage.

She didn't need to erase the past to move forward. She needed to forgive herself for *not knowing what she couldn't yet see*. To forgive the silence, the self-abandonment, the waiting for someone else to choose her. She whispered the most vital truth of all:

"I didn't deserve what happened to me—but I also don't deserve to keep carrying it."

That was the moment she knew: The apology she'd been waiting for wasn't from them. It was from her. And she finally said it.

⚠ Sidebar: Signs You're Stuck in Self-Condemnation

You might be punishing yourself instead of forgiving yourself if:

- You replay the same mistakes in your mind.
- You speak to yourself in ways you'd never speak to someone you care about.
- You shrink back because you don't trust yourself anymore.
- You define your worth by what you failed to do.
- You carry shame for choices made in confusion, not clarity.
- You feel undeserving of rest, grace, or a fresh start.

From Condemnation → Regret → Grace → Growth

Think of self-forgiveness as a progression. It's not instant, but a journey that moves you from self-punishment toward freedom.

- **Condemnation:** "I am what I did."
    - Shame and self-punishment keep you stuck in the wound.
- **Regret:** "I wish I had chosen differently."
    - Honest acknowledgment of harm, without self-erasure.
- **Grace:** "I see my mistake, but I still see my worth."
    - Releasing yourself from the endless debt of punishment.
- **Growth:** "I've learned, and I'll live differently."
    - Using clarity as a compass, not a weapon.

Self-forgiveness isn't denial. It's the choice to stop being your own jailer.

* * *

What Refinement Looks Like Throughout the Spectrum

Refinement doesn't look the same for everyone. It depends on how deep the wound goes and where you stand on the spectrum of forgiveness.

● Minor Annoyances

- **Clarity (the fire):** Noticing when minor irritations pile up.
- **Refinement (forgiveness):** Choosing release over scorekeeping.

◉ Patterns of Disregard

- **Clarity (the fire):** Recognizing repeated boundary-crossing or disrespect.
- **Refinement (forgiveness):** Letting go of the illusion they'll change without evidence—and adjusting how you engage.

◉ Serious or Chronic Harm

- **Clarity (the fire):** Naming abuse or betrayal without denial.
- **Refinement (forgiveness):** Refusing to carry bitterness—without excusing the harm and releasing the wound's grip, with or without reconciliation.

At every stage, **clarity is the fire that reveals truth**. **Forgiveness is the refinement** that shapes what remains—determining whether you'll step into thriving or stay trapped in survival.

* * *

Refined by the Fire: The Final Test of Clarity

Framing Thought: The fire isn't here to destroy you—it's here to define you. What survives the burn was never fragile. What falls away was never meant to carry forward. Clarity exposes what's real. Forgiveness refines what remains. Together, they form the crucible where truth, integrity, and peace are forged—not without pain, but with purpose. This is where you begin sorting. Not everything gets to take the journey with you.

What has clarity stripped away from me?

Clarity removes illusion. It reveals what was real—and what you only hoped was. It shows you who someone is, not who you wish they were. You may find yourself letting go of:

- The illusion that loyalty fixes dysfunction.
- The fantasy that love alone will change someone.
- The mask of being "the strong one."
- The guilt of choosing peace over performance.
- The belief that forgiveness must include reunion.

Clarity clears the emotional clutter, allowing you to stop performing and start healing.

After the fire, what is worth holding on to—and what must I release?

This question isn't about loss—it's about discernment. What stays must serve your peace, your growth, and your integrity. Hold on to:

- Boundaries that protect your energy.
- Lessons that came with pain—but not the pain itself.
- People who show up with respect, even in disagreement.
- The version of you that feels grounded and whole.

Release:

- The need for closure from the unwilling.
- Guilt that kept you in cycles of self-betrayal.
- Stories that cast you as too much—or never enough.
- The urge to justify your healing to those committed to misunderstanding it.

Where am I still resisting refinement because the truth feels too heavy to face?

Some truths are heavy because they ask us to let go of what once felt like home—even when it hurt. Refinement means facing those truths anyway. You might be resisting if:

- You keep explaining someone's harm instead of naming it.
- You delay a boundary that your peace is already begging for.
- You cling to an identity you've outgrown because change feels disloyal.

Framing Thought: Resistance often blocks the doorway to healing—yet it's also the very signpost showing you where the work begins."

* * *

Emotional Arc—Chapter 11: Discerning Forgiveness

Core Tension

You've been told forgiveness is simple—automatic, instant, universal. But deep down, you know it's more layered than that. You've experienced wounds that didn't resolve with time, silence, or surface-level words. You've wrestled with resentment, guilt, and pressure—wondering if you're bitter for still hurting, or "cold-hearted" for holding your distance.

Clarity reveals what you hadn't fully named: betrayal, disconnection, harm caused by others, and harm done to yourself. The fire of truth burns away the denial—but it also leaves you exposed, grieving, and asking: *What now?*

Positive Balance

The "what now" is refinement. Clarity shows that forgiveness isn't one-size-fits-all. It lives on a spectrum. Some moments call for mercy; others require boundaries. Some relationships recover; others release. You begin to see that forgiveness is a principled choice, not a pressured performance. It's not about pretending it didn't happen—it's about refusing to let it define you. Forgiveness becomes a practice of courage, not concession.

Rigid formulas or forced timelines no longer bind you. You're invited to explore forgiveness *with discernment*—grounded in truth, led by clarity, and guided by wisdom. You don't have to return to what hurt you to release what no longer serves you.

Empowerment

This is where freedom lives. You reclaim agency—not in isolation, but in alignment with truth and peace. You now understand that:

- **Forgiveness is not erasure.**
- **Mercy can coexist with boundaries.**
- **Compassion doesn't require reunion.**
- **Letting go doesn't mean forgetting—it means freeing.**

This is where freedom lives. You're no longer trapped by black-and-white rules or pressure to pretend. You have a compass. A spectrum. Permission to forgive on your terms. Now, forgiveness becomes a source of strength—not a surrender. It's how you honor truth without staying bound to pain. It's how you move forward without dragging what was never yours to carry.

You no longer confuse endurance with love, or silence with maturity. Forgiveness becomes a daily decision to let go of what was never yours to hold. You stop equating reconciliation with moral superiority—and start seeing wholeness as the objective measure of growth.

Whether directed toward others or yourself, forgiveness becomes an act of integrity. It's not about finding the "right way"—it's about choosing the path that honors truth, preserves your peace, and aligns with your values. Refinement doesn't mean you're over it. It means you're no longer under its control. You're walking forward—defined by the positive things that endured, not by what tried to break you.

* * *

Chapter 11 Summary and Closing: Discerning Forgiveness

Forgiveness is not the end of the story—it's the turning point. Once you've walked through the fire of clarity and chosen growth, you can't unsee what's been revealed. You can't return to the illusion that "forgive and forget" is always noble, or that reconciliation should be pursued at any cost. That version of you—the one who confused peacekeeping with peace—is gone.

This kind of forgiveness requires courage. It asks you to be honest about what happened, to carry dignity even in your wounds, and to release the bitterness or shame that was never yours to hold. It doesn't demand public declarations or confrontations. The work is internal—and that shift within you quietly changes how you move in the world.

Forgiveness doesn't erase what happened. It affirms that you lived through it. And survival, while essential, was never the final destination. Survival was the starting point. Forgiveness gives you more than relief from the past—it grants you strength for what's ahead. It clears the debris so the road can rise to meet you.

Forgiveness is the doorway, not the destination. On the other side is your true self—steadier, freer, still unfolding. But unfolding requires more than clarity alone. It requires a lens that doesn't distort, diminish, or demand perfection. A way of seeing that reshapes old beliefs and aligns you with your truest design.

✦ Chapter 11: Discerning Forgiveness – Pause for Perspective

Virtue: Mercy

According to lexicographer Gesenius, the Hebrew root of *mercy* suggests "a gentle emotion of mind." That definition matters—because clarity always begins in the mind. It dares you to think differently, to name what's been hidden, and to confront what was once too painful to admit. But that mental shift doesn't come cheap. You've paid for it in grief, in fear, in anger and resentment, in guilt and silence.

Mercy brings softness to a mind that has carried too much weight. It steadies the hand that now holds truth. Because clarity without mercy can cut too sharply—injuring you and others in its pursuit of justice. But with mercy, truth becomes precision. It becomes a scalpel, not a sword. It removes what no longer serves without destroying what's still sacred. Mercy is what keeps clarity from turning into cynicism. It transforms emotional cost into emotional capacity.

The goal of this book has never been to tell you that clarity is easy—it isn't. Clarity comes at the cost of comfort, illusion, and sometimes connection. But with mercy, the cost becomes a catalyst. What could have broken you instead shapes you. What could have hardened you instead frees you. What could have turned your heart cold instead teaches it tenderness.

Clarity begins in the mind. Mercy decides how you carry it in your heart. Together, they prepare you:

- For the mirror.
- For the mountain.
- For what's next.

☞ Next Steps: Workbook Journal Prompts

For deeper reflection on this stage of *Discerning Forgiveness*, turn to the Companion Workbook for Chapter 11. Use the prompts to explore how grief and accountability shape your definition of forgiveness, where refinement is asking you to release or preserve, and how mercy can steady the emotional cost of clarity.

 ## Personal Notes & Insights

Use this page to capture any quotes, ideas, or personal revelations that surfaced while reading. Let it be messy, real, and yours.

_____

_____

_____

_____

_____

_____

_____

_____

_____

_____

_____

_____

_____

_____

THE EMOTIONAL COST OF CLARITY

TO THE MIRROR AND THE MOUNTAIN

The mirror reflects. The mountain reveals.

You were a mirror reflecting the power I hadn't yet claimed and the pain I hadn't yet healed. In your presence, I had to face myself: not just the version I showed, but the truth beneath the patterns, the people-pleasing, and my definitions of love, happiness, and success—a success built on survival.

And still, you were a mountain—a climb through unexpectedly turbulent terrain. A path I chose when my thinking was clouded, and my emotions were unsteady. A hike that reflected who I was then—but not who I am becoming now. For a while, I resented that climb. But resentment has loosened its grip. In its place, gratitude has taken root—gratitude for the clarity gained from navigating such rugged terrain.

Thanks to clarity, I didn't just survive the climb; I grew stronger because of it. You are no longer the mirror that will affirm me. I stopped letting this mountain path define me. Your approval was never the pinnacle to reach. Our paths are no longer the same. The path I now choose leads to a higher, more elevated summit—a mountain aligned with truth, stewardship, faith, hope, and wisdom.

A path that leads to true fulfillment, not superficial success. It is the path I hope this book encourages others to follow.

With clarity,
Shante

CHAPTER 12
THE MIRROR AND THE MOUNTAIN

Clarity guides you. Wisdom propels you.

Letting go of 'a connection that didn't serve you wasn't just about releasing a person—it was about confronting the mindset that led you there in the first place. That's what clarity does. It doesn't just reveal the mountain you've climbed; it forces you to face the beliefs and emotions that convinced you to make that climb at all. This book has been your mirror. Page after page, it has reflected your patterns to you: the ways you've thought, felt, and acted—often from survival rather than alignment. But a mirror only matters if you respond to what it shows.

That is the challenge now. Will you glance at your reflection and keep moving as if nothing has shifted? Or will you let what you've seen here guide you toward a new path—one that elevates your principles, your choices, and your direction, grounded in truth, practical wisdom, and accountability? Because clarity was never just about seeing differently, it was always about living differently.

* * *

Pillar 1: The Mirror Reveals Your Thinking

Looking in the mirror almost always begins with a trigger—a reason you glance at your reflection in the first place. Maybe you're preparing for an event, heading to work, or someone quietly points out something on your face. Something prompts you to check.

But here's the other side: you can often tell when someone avoids the mirror. They rush past their reflection, hoping not to notice. Over time, that neglect shows. It appears in the details they miss, how they present themselves, and how they show up for others. The same is true internally. When we don't pause to reflect honestly, it doesn't stay hidden. It manifests in our choices, our relationships, and the way we carry ourselves in the world.

Once you're in front of the mirror, the first thing you do is identify the facts of what you see:

- A smudge across your cheek.
- A matching outfit.
- Lipstick on your teeth.
- A hair out of place.
- Well-executed makeup.

At this stage, the mirror is neutral. It simply reflects what is. But the longer you look, those facts start to form thoughts:

- A smudge becomes "I should have caught that sooner."
- Lipstick on your teeth becomes "Why don't I pay more attention?"
- A well-selected outfit becomes "I look professional today."

The facts stay neutral, but the thoughts you attach to them do not. You've already done this type of mirror work in the early chapters of this book. Each acted as a reflection of your thinking—surfacing misconceptions you may have carried for years:

Guarded Giving (Chapter 1): The false belief that over-functioning proved your love—that being constantly needed was the same as being valued.

Boundary Building (Chapter 2): The misconception that saying "no" meant letting people down—and that disappointing others automatically meant rejection.

Redefining Love (Chapter 3): The mistaken belief that unconditional devotion always equals healthy love—even when it demands silence, sacrifice, or survival.

Respect and Self-Betrayal (Chapter 4): The distorted idea that humility required erasing yourself—that being "peaceful" meant tolerating disrespect or remaining quiet while your worth was diminished.

Each chapter held up the mirror—not to flatter you, but to reveal the hidden drivers in your thinking.

Stop here.

The purpose of this first pillar was not to fix anything yet—not to erase the smudge or reapply the lipstick. It was to notice the connection between seeing and thinking. To practice honesty about what showed up in the mirror—and sincerity about the thoughts it revealed in you.

Clarity began with your willingness to acknowledge reality.

* * *

Pillar 2: The Mirror Reveals Your Feelings

When you stand in front of a mirror, the first layer is straightforward: the facts. Then you add your thoughts about those facts. But the mirror doesn't stop there. The longer you gaze, the more those thoughts begin to stir something deeper. They awaken emotion.

Think about it.

- You notice a smudge on your face (fact). You think *I should have caught that sooner* (thought). Then the feeling rises—embarrassment, even a sting of self-consciousness: *People must think I don't care. Maybe I'm careless.*
- You notice lipstick on your teeth (fact). You think, *Pay more attention* (thought). Then comes the emotion—shame mixed with regret: *Everyone must have seen it before I did. I look unprepared.*
- You see, your makeup is well applied (fact). You think *My face really pops today* (thought). The feelings that follow are pride and confidence, along with a hint of excitement: *Today, someone is going to notice me.*
- You notice your outfit matches well (fact). You think *I look professional today* (thought). The feeling that follows is confidence, tinged with anticipation: *Maybe today, I'll be taken seriously.*

The mirror isn't solely about your appearance; it also reflects how your thoughts stir emotion. These feelings, in turn, often drive your next steps. You encountered this emotional mirror earlier in the second part of this book, where each chapter encouraged you to confront the emotions beneath your thoughts:

Emotional Availability and the Fear of Being Felt (Chapter 5): Revealed the fear behind the thought, *If I open up, I'll be hurt.* The emotions that followed were anxiety, insecurity, and guardedness. Yet alongside them came relief in naming your need and courage in taking small risks to be seen.

Gratitude and Resentment (Chapter 6): Highlighted the conflict between the mind's command to "be thankful" despite harm and the reality of growing bitterness. The tension exposed frustration, guilt, and hidden anger. Yet gratitude also offered moments of peace, acceptance, and even contentment—proof that resentment didn't have the final say.

Performative Connection (Chapter 7): Unearthed the ache beneath the thought, *If I perform, I'll belong.* The feelings that followed were emptiness, disillusionment, and quiet grief. But breaking free from performance brought empowerment, relief, and the joy of showing up authentically.

Emotional Safety and Intimacy (Chapter 8): Invited you to admit that some connections weren't as genuine as you'd hoped. The emotions were disappointment, sadness, and loneliness. Yet alongside those complex feelings came longing and anticipation—the yearning for spaces where consistency, care, and trust could make vulnerability safe again.

Each of these chapters acted as a mirror, showing you not only what you were thinking but also how those thoughts made you feel. And those feelings were not neutral. They shaped how you acted, withdrew, performed, trusted, or protected yourself. That's the essence of this second pillar: thoughts never exist in isolation. They always carry emotion. And as you begin to notice the feelings beneath your thoughts, you also start to understand why you've made the choices you've made.

Stop here.

This second pillar isn't about choosing your next move. It's about pausing long enough to name the emotions beneath the surface.

Clarity doesn't just ask, *What do I see?* It also asks, *How do I feel about what I see?*

This is what I call **The Emotional Cost of Clarity**™.

It's the toll you've paid to deepen your understanding of how you show up in life. The purpose of this book wasn't only to reveal your thinking—it was to challenge the long-standing beliefs you've lived under. Looking in the mirror and daring to question those beliefs came at a cost.

This has not been an easy journey. You've felt frustration, disillusionment, regret, insecurity, guilt, and even anger. Those emotions surfaced in the ache of thoughts colliding with truth. But that cost wasn't wasted—it proved you've been doing the hard work of seeing yourself honestly.

And now you stand here with the return on your investment. Clarity made you pay in painful emotion, but it also gave you something greater: the first glimpse of wisdom—the ability to think differently, feel differently, and begin to live differently.

* * *

Pillar 3: Choosing Your Mountain (Your Actions)

Looking in the mirror can reveal your thoughts and stir your feelings. But for wisdom to take root, it must move you into action. What you do with what you've seen becomes the most accurate reflection of your clarity. That's what we've called throughout this book: *clarity in motion.*

The mirror shows you facts.

Your thoughts interpret them.

Your feelings intensify them.

But the steps you take next—the actions you choose—shape the road you walk and the mountain you climb. Think about it:

- You notice a smudge on your face. You think *I should have caught that sooner.* You feel uneasy. So, you wipe it off and continue.
- You see lipstick on your teeth. You think, *Pay more attention.* You feel self-conscious. So, you correct it, and the way forward looks different from what it would have been if you had ignored it.
- You see that your outfit matches well. You think *I look professional today.* You feel confident. So, you carry yourself with presence and strength.

Every small action becomes a step. Each step forms a path. And every path leads to a mountain. Some mountains are false peaks—built on fear, survival, performance, or the need for approval. You can climb them, but once you reach the top, the view leaves you hollow. But there is also a higher, more authentic summit—a mountain grounded in truth, courage, hope, stewardship, and wisdom. The terrain may still be rough, but the reward is peace, purpose, and a success you can sustain.

You've already practiced this "choosing" in the last chapters:

Isolating Reconnection (Chapter 9): Choosing distance as a step toward peace instead of walking the path of self-betrayal.

The Space in Between (Chapter 10): Choosing patience to climb the mountain of conviction instead of sliding back into old patterns for short-term comfort.

Discerning Forgiveness (Chapter 11): Choosing to release what burdens you to ascend the mountain of freedom instead of carrying resentment that only exhausts you.

Each of these chapters revealed one truth: the mountain you reach is determined by the path you choose. Clarity invites you to take the route that may feel harder at first but leads to greater fulfillment in the long run.

That's the essence of this third pillar: the mirror revealed your thoughts, the second pillar exposed your feelings, and now wisdom compels you to act—to choose a better path, and therefore, a better mountain.

Stop here.

Clarity now asks: *Where will you walk next, and which mountain will you climb?*

This is why the final chapter is titled *The Mirror and the Mountain.* The mirror revealed the truths you can no longer avoid. The mountain represents the destination shaped by your choices. You've seen the cost of chasing counterfeit peaks. You've felt the ache of false success. But now, clarity challenges you to choose differently.

This is your turning point—let wisdom guide your steps toward a higher, steadier, and more peace-filled summit.

* * *

Pullout Story: A Mirror in the Boardroom

One of my clients, a high-achieving executive, came to me utterly drained. On paper, she had it all—the degree, the title, the salary, the house, the family, and the admiration of her colleagues. But when she looked in the mirror, she didn't see pride. She saw a woman running on fumes, struggling to recognize herself beyond the roles she played.

Her mirror moment came during a team retreat. In a rare flash of honesty, she confessed, "I don't even know if the version of me they admire is the real me anymore. I'm chasing things I don't even value. They were things I was told I should want."

That realization cut deep. The emotions that followed were heavier still—grief for the years she spent performing, resentment for the expectations she carried, and fear of what might unravel if she stopped.

Then came the choice. She could keep climbing the mountain of performance and approval—or risk the more challenging, truer climb. Over time, she chose the latter. She began aligning her actions with her values, speaking candidly in meetings, and letting her "no" carry weight again. Yes, she lost a few admirers—but she regained her authenticity. And with it, her peace.

Her story captures the heart of this book: the mirror exposes your truth, your emotions reveal the cost, and the mountain is defined by the path you choose next. She chose alignment over applause—a steeper climb, but one that restored her self-respect, her clarity, and a success she could finally call her own.

* * *

꩜ Emotional Arc – Chapter 12: The Mirror and the Mountain

Core Tension

You've paid the price of clarity through the intense emotions that surfaced as your old thoughts and beliefs began to collapse. You've been carrying the ache of what clarity exposed, and now the tension is this: *What will I do with the clarity I now possess?*

Positive Balance

Pillar 1 (Thinking): Awareness brought discomfort. Naming facts and confronting the thoughts behind them revealed distortions and survival-based definitions of success. You felt exposed and uneasy, but also challenged. The process of change had begun.

Pillar 2 (Feeling): Your thoughts triggered painful yet hopeful emotions. You sat beneath the weight of *The Emotional Cost of Clarity,* but also began to see the return on your investment: insight and discernment taking root.

Pillar 3 (Acting): You faced the challenge of turning awareness into action. When clarity shifts from reflection to action, it guides you toward a truer, more meaningful summit.

Empowered

The mirror reflected and challenged your thoughts, beliefs, and emotions. Success has been redefined—no longer measured by survival, but by stewardship and purpose, seen through the lens of contentment, patience, discernment, and peace. Wisdom has become your return on investment.

You now hold the privilege and responsibility of choosing your mountain. Choose one that truly honors your values—and benefits the life you're building.

* * *

The Emotional Cost of Clarity Closing Summary

Clarity was your goal. Grief, frustration, and longing were the costs you paid. Wisdom is the return on that investment. The mirror revealed what you could no longer deny—your thoughts, beliefs, patterns, and the emotions they stirred. The mountain showed that your actions, choices, and direction determine the summit you reach.

Each chapter has led you here:

Guarded Giving, Boundary Building, Redefining Love, and **Respect & Betrayal** challenged your beliefs. **Emotional Availability, Gratitude & Resentment, Performative Connection,** and **Emotional Safety** uncovered the feelings beneath them. **Isolating Reconnection, The Space in Between,** and **Discerning Forgiveness** revealed what happens when those insights begin shaping your actions. Now, **The Mirror and the Mountain** place a choice before you:

- Will you keep climbing the false peaks of performance, approval, and survival?
- Or will you choose a truer summit—one rooted in stewardship, alignment, peace, and purpose?

This journey has not been easy. You've shed tears, faced betrayals, endured losses, and carried truths that felt unbearable. That was the toll of clarity. Yet through it all, wisdom has taken root. Clarity didn't just shift your perspective—it reshaped how you think, feel, and live. And that is the breakthrough:

- A redefined vision of success.
- A more intentional path.
- The awareness to know when the mountain you're climbing truly matters.

Clarity is not just about escaping survival mode—it's about embracing a new way of seeing. It's about thriving. That is the safeguard of practical wisdom: it doesn't erase the ache, but it steadies your steps, protects your choices, and preserves your energy—so you don't lose yourself on mountains never worth the climb. So the final question is yours to answer:

What is it costing me to climb the mountain I'm on—and am I ready to choose a different path?

✦ Chapter 12: The Mirror and the Mountain – Pause for Perspective

Virtue: Wisdom

Wisdom isn't just knowing the difference between right and wrong—it's living that difference in a way that honors truth. It's practical, grounded, and deeply human. It shows itself not in what you can recite, but in how you apply what you've learned. It rejects hollow comfort and empty advice. Real wisdom steadies, supports, and empowers. It becomes a refuge, not another burden to carry.

Wisdom also pushes back against counterfeit success. It resists chasing applause, roles, or distractions, and instead centers on care, presence, and responsibility with what's already in your hands. Practical wisdom chooses healing over dazzling—what endures over what fades. And wisdom always looks forward. It doesn't stop at what feels good in the moment; it considers impact, consequence, and the legacy of your choices. It knows that some mountains aren't worth climbing, no matter how impressive they appear from a distance.

The emotional cost of clarity brought you here—but wisdom ensures that cost wasn't wasted. It reminds you that you cannot carry fear and courage at the same time, nor can you cling to performance while reaching for authenticity.

In the end, you must decide: *Which mountain will you climb?*

Wisdom guides that choice. It protects your strength, steadies your steps, and keeps your path aligned with your values. This is how clarity lifts you beyond survival—into a life where you can truly thrive.

The next chapter of your becoming begins here—learning who you are beyond labels, roles, and survival habits.

☞ Next Steps: Workbook Journal Prompts

For deeper reflection on how wisdom shapes your thoughts, emotions, and actions — and how it helps you choose a mountain you actually value — turn to the Companion Workbook for Chapter 12.

 **Personal Notes & Insights**

Use this page to capture any quotes, ideas, or personal revelations that surfaced while reading. Let it be messy, real, and yours.

_____

_____

_____

_____

_____

_____

_____

_____

_____

_____

_____

_____

_____

_____

_____

_____

_____

AFTER THE CLARITY

Before you read this final reflection, I want to share something you should be aware of. When my own clarity first deepened, I couldn't turn it off. I saw brokenness everywhere—in people, in systems, and in myself. I scrutinized everything and everyone. I carried judgment in my heart, unconsciously. What began as clarity slowly hardened into criticism—and left unchecked, could have turned into self-righteousness.

This piece, *After Clarity*, was written as a reminder. A reminder to myself—and now to you—that clarity is a gift, but it's not meant to harden us. It's meant to free us. Don't let it become something you can't stop pounding, like a gavel. You can recognize harm without constantly reliving its history. You can see someone for who they are—and still choose peace instead of dwelling on their potential. You can let go of the need to be justified or validated and reclaim your right to freedom.

Discernment doesn't require that you stay angry—only that you stay awake. So let judgment rest. Let grace return, not for them, but for the parts of you still holding court long after the case was closed. Because clarity isn't just about what you see—it's about what you're finally ready to let go.

After the clarity,
Shante

A FINAL LETTER TO YOU

You made it.

Through the pain, the questions, the mirror, and the mountains—you stayed. You read. You wrestled. You reflected. And that alone proves your strength.

Clarity has cost you something. It always does. But now you see that the cost was never wasted. Every tear, every pause, every quiet decision to keep turning the page has been building something within you—wisdom, alignment, and the courage to make different choices.

You don't need to have all the answers right now. You don't need the whole map. Just keep moving toward what's true. Keep honoring the small steps. Keep tending the seeds of peace, purpose, and freedom you've planted here. And when you forget, look in the mirror. Recall what you've seen. Remember what you've felt. Then choose the mountain worth climbing.

You are not alone in this. Many powerful women are releasing outdated definitions of success, old ways of being, and false ideals. You are part of a greater story—one of people choosing clarity over confusion, alignment over approval, and wisdom over performance.

So keep going. Not perfectly. Not urgently. Just faithfully—one clear step at a time. Because clarity has never been about perfection. It's always been about your right to thrive.

Clarified,
Shante

ABOUT THE AUTHOR

Shante Alexander, MA, PCC, is an Organizational Psychologist, ICF-credentialed executive coach, and Gallup-certified strengths coach. She works with leaders, teams, and high-performing professionals through coaching, facilitation, and strategic workshops focused on burnout, identity, and sustainable leadership.

Across corporate, nonprofit, and public-sector environments, Shante is known for challenging high achievers to examine the patterns that once made them successful — and question whether those patterns are still serving them. Her work addresses performance culture, over-responsibility, and the hidden cost of being indispensable.

Blending psychological science, strengths-based development, and lived experience, she guides individuals and organizations through the discomfort of clarity toward intentional redesign.

If *The Emotional Cost of Clarity™* resonated with you, there is more waiting beyond these pages.

Explore additional reflections, speaking events, and resources designed to support your continued growth.

Visit: www.shantealexander.com

www.ingramcontent.com/pod-product-compliance
Lightning Source LLC
LaVergne TN
LVHW021232080526
838199LV00088B/4320